The Survival of Love

The Loving Light Books Series

Book 1: God Spoke through Me to Tell You to Speak to Him
Book 2 & 3: No One Will Listen to God & You are God
Book 4: The Sun and Beyond
Book 5: The Neverending Love of God
Book 6: The Survival of Love
Book 7: We All Go Together
Book 8: God's Imagination
Book 9: Forever God
Book 10: See the Light
Book 11: Your Life as God
Book 12: God Lives
Book 13: The Realization of Creation
Book 14: Illumination
Book 15: I Touched God
Book 16: I and God are One
Book 17: We All Walk Together
Book 18: Love Conquers All
Book 19: Come to the Light of Love
Book 20: The Grace is Ours

Also by Liane Rich

The Book of Love
For the Love of God: An Introduction to God
For the Love of Money: Creating Your Personal Reality
Your Individual Divinity: Existing in Parallel Realities
For the Love of Life on Earth
Your Return to the Light of Love: a guidebook to spiritual awakening

Loving Light

Book 6

The Survival of Love

Liane Rich

The information contained in this book is not intended as a substitute for professional medical advice. Neither the publisher nor the author is engaged in rendering professional advice to the reader. The remedies and suggestions in this book should not be taken, or construed, as standard medical diagnosis, prescription or treatment. For any medical issue or illness consult a qualified physician.

Loving Light Books

ISBN 13: 978-1-878480-06-4
ISBN 10: 1-878480-06-5

Loving Light Books:
www.lovinglightbooks.com

Also Available at:
Amazon: www.amazon.com
Barnes & Noble: www.barnesandnoble.com

for Peter and Karen

The information in this series is not necessarily meant to be taken literally. It is meant to *shift* your consciousness....

Foreword

Anyone immersed in the vast body of new metaphysical knowledge is aware of the virtual symphony of voices from channeled sources throughout the world – inspirational voices that may be artistic, poetic, philosophical, religious, or scientific. And now, out of these myriad New Age voices, comes a series of books by God, channeled through Liane, revealing the frank truth in all its glory and wonder, telling us how to cleanse our bodies, gain access to our subconscious minds, clear our other selves and march back to who we are – God.

In God's books you will be introduced to a loving, powerful, gripping, exciting, and often humorous voice that reaches out and speaks ever so personally to the individual reader. As the reader's interest deepens, invariably an intimate relationship to this voice develops. It is a relationship that lasts forever, and I am quite certain I do mean forever.

Here is an accelerated program, a no-holds-barred course, where God guides us and loves us, and as needs be recommends books to us and even a movie or musical piece along the way. He (She) enters our lives and sees through our eyes, seeming to enjoy the ride as He guides us back to US, back to ALL. Here is a voice that is playful and informative, that is humorous and serious, that is gentle and powerfully divine. It is a voice that knows no barriers or restrictions, a straightforward and honest voice that caresses us when we need the warmth and pushes us when we are immobilized.

In today's New Age literature there is an avalanche of information from magnificent beings of light, information that possesses us and compels us to look at our fears and express our love. In this series of books by God, you will find truly powerful methods for making this transition from toxicity to purity, from density to light, from fear to love, and from the delusion of death to the awakening to full life. You will experience in these books the love and the power of God for it is your love to express and your power to behold. Rarely will you see more lucid steps for transformation. Read these beautiful words and rejoice in our period of awakening, our return to Home.

John Farrell, PhD., LCSW. – Psychologist, Clinical Social Worker, Senior Clinician Psychiatric Emergency Services, U.C. Davis Medical Center, Sacramento. John is also a retired Professor – California State University, Sacramento, in Health Sciences and Psychology.

The Survival of Love

Introduction

So far we have not been able to stop war on planet earth. War must stop. It is not simply a time to love; it is also a time to stop anger and resistance. Resistance creates all pain. Once you begin to resist, you begin to hold-on to a thought process that says, "No, this is not right," or "This is bad." We will learn in this book how to survive love. Love is not in danger so much as our desire to love. Desire to love has lost balance. Most love is appreciated only when received and most love is received and then returned unused.

You do not love out of longing as you believe. Love is meant to be for you. *You must learn to love you.* Never allow love to die. If you do, you will die. You are love and you are not meant to be fear. Each time that you decide to forego a relationship because you feel threatened, you are killing off your love of you. You are not the one who will suffer in the end. God will continue no matter what you decide, however you will kill love.

Love is continuous only as long as light exists. In the beginning you came from light and you return to light. Once you begin to refrain from war and violence and vengeance, you will once again be light.

You have spent such a great amount of energy destroying who you are that you may never again recapture all of you. Your mission on earth is not so simple as you believe. You are not simply here to begin to see how you contain love and light. You are here because you chose to come at this time. Those who have evolved to a state of complete awareness (on certain levels) have chosen to interfere in death at this time. *Death and destruction are illusion.* They do not exist and I do not wish you to believe "in" them.

What you believe "in" is what you create. You must begin to believe in God. God is light and God is love and God does not die… not ever. Once you begin to accept this as fact, you will become light awareness and ascend. Believe it and it is. It is so simple. Do not spend your time believing in doom. All doom and chaos are to end now. I do not wish to override your will, but I am asking you to put down your guns and put anger to rest and start to love me.

I will wish to show you how you too may survive this chaos that you believe to exist on planet earth. It is all fabricated and staged just as your movies that you so eagerly pay to see. You are spending your money to see exactly what souls see when they watch you. They know the prop man placed the dynamite to blow a hole in his fake mountain, and they know the make-up artist painted blood to frighten and scare the wits out of you. You do not die. No one kills and you are not killing planet earth. She is not real and you are not real. You are energy and she is energy and soon you will begin to see how all works and *is*. For now, I wish to welcome you back for another enlightening and informative session. I am ready to teach my sixth graders their lessons. No more beating around the bush. We are all adults now and we each know how to love and how to not control others. Let's start with love and acceptance of all, and we will be well on our way to graduating from this sixth grade class.

So far you have learned a great deal from my first five books. For those of you who were drawn to this, our sixth book, I suggest you begin with Book One which is titled, *God Spoke through Me to Tell You to Speak to Him.* I have been writing books through this particular channel for some time now and she believes that I am God. I wish her to know that *I Am.* She will find it necessary to convince others, but of course that's life on planet earth. Better put, "that's life on this particular set or stage." You see, there are other dramas being acted out in other areas of this galaxy and even in other universes. This particular drama is based on a very good story, and I am the only one who knows how this story will end. You see, I am

God and I will tell you how you turn around hatred and anger and control and guilt and even love. You *will* change and you will rise up and be God – no big deal really. I wrote the play and I'm playing all your parts. You are really not you. You are really me. Stop pretending to be you and begin to be God.

This show is good, but we are in the last act and last scene and it's curtain time. Wake up and know that your show is ending and you are going to take off your costume and come back with me. Back home!

God

You do not believe that you are God and this is how I will convince you. I will begin with the human form and continue to clear and clean until you are open. Once I see that you are open, I will begin to move in. Once I move in you will receive information more readily and you may even begin to realize how you are indeed God.

So far you have done well in your studies and you have not been harmed in any way. God does not cause pain, he only clears pain. Most of you are so afraid of me that you do not wish to communicate freely with me. If I were to speak with you freely and openly, you would most likely run and hide from me or be afraid that I knew how bad you had been all your life, and your guilt would create greater fear. Liane refused to speak with me out of her fear that I was going to punish her for all her sins. When she would not speak to me, I sent Archangel Michael on my behalf. He woke her in the middle of her sleep and asked that she please communicate with God. He did not have much success as she rudely told him to go away. She didn't trust that he was who he said he was, and she didn't wish to be frightened further. Michael left immediately as he did not wish to frighten her further. He was not to interfere in any way and she did not wish his presence.

This is how all works. Ask and you shall receive. Ask for angels to guide and protect and they will be there for you. Lock your doors and bolt your bolts, and stop pretending to be safe and you upset the balance. You left angels behind to guide and protect you. They are part of you and you left them where you could use them most.

Often angels do not wish to be rude so they simply let you lead your own life. You put them in position in order to have balance. You wished to keep part of you out of this plane and have a strong guide from beyond. Now you bolt and lock and hide and it is not balance. How can you put part of you in another dimension and not allow them to do the work that you asked them to do? It is most unusual to hire someone for a job and then not trust or allow them the opportunity to do what they are hired to do.

You will find that most of you do not allow your angels to do the least little thing for you. You not only do not allow them to be with you, you do not allow them to protect you, nor to love you, nor to do this protecting job that you have hired them for. So, what I would like is to see each and every one of you begin to love your angels. Love them enough to allow them to be your guides and protectors. I do not have work for them here in heaven and they are bored. Please allow them to come back to you and become part of you once again. They do not wish to be left outside of you any longer.

Allow all to be as it was planned. Do not be so frightened of voices from outside of you. You are so vast and so scattered and so magnificent that you will be in awe when you finally discover your true identity. You are God. Stop pretending to be human. There is a plan here and this plan is to come home in your finest state of being. You left God only to return to God. God decided to take a good look at himself and he could not look from within. He worked out a way in which he could return out of love but he never left. He is God within God. He is all that is. He changed part of himself in order to see more of creation.

How can I look at me when I am me? I decided to step out of me, only there is no way to get out of God because God is all. So I took it upon myself to create a way in which I could view myself. This became the plan and you are the part of God who volunteered. It's a good plan. Step out of God to look at God and see how vast he really is. This could be put simpler… step out of character and become what you are not in order to see what you really are. Change who you are so you may reflect back on the greatness of what you once were.

How often do you think of youth and its wonders and how fit you were and tireless and even humorous?

Now you are tired and bored and there is not so much humor in your life. You look back and really appreciate what you once were. Only now you long to be youthful again. Well, this is my plan – long for godliness by missing God. You are all missing God. You volunteered to change to another form in order to look back at God so that God could see how good it is to "be" God.

You do not wish to be alone in this big world so I am now telling you how I am you. You have come to a place that is most uncomfortable to you and I can help. Push me out of you if you must, but I will return. You have never been left alone. You are not "in" body, as darkness and debris have taken charge. You are now guiding from outside and you no longer care what happens "within" you or within form. Form is being left to die and it is creating confusion for you. You do not wish to stay and you do not wish to leave. Most of you do not wish to leave at death and yet you create death to escape earth and its rules.

You decide to reincarnate and then you forget it's you, and you begin to believe you are flesh and so you kill you by trying to destroy your own bodies – you put so much poison into you that it is spilling forth onto others and now you can actually contaminate one another. How do you breathe a cold from one form, or body, to another when there really is no such disease? *All* disease is mental. It starts at a psychological level and works its way to a body level then you begin to wash your throat and clear your lungs and your body begins to believe that this cold really is.

Most of you are so *convincing* with your rules that you now "catch" cold once or twice a year and of course it's right on schedule. Stop creating more illness. Clean up your own messes and you will begin to clean up your planet. When you have cleaned you to the point that you no longer *receive* colds from your own thoughts, I will be very happy.

Go in peace, God bless you and your world, and please learn to clean up your own messes. They begin in your mind. It is a belief in control that harms the most and often lack of control will lead to stress. Let go of stress by "letting go and letting God." No more asking for what you want. Ask for what God wants *for* you and then accept it and flow with it.

*I*n the beginning you did not wish to be in form. You began to leave your body and travel without it. Now I am going to teach you to stay “in” body and travel with it. You have been letting body go for so long that it no longer suits you to stay within form. Most of you complain of aches and pains and age. I will tell you now that you do not age and the only aches and pains you will receive are given to you, by you. You began to wake up to the fact that body is not you and you left. You took the easy way out because you did not wish to learn to operate you.

Most of you are like children in school. When the going gets tough, you skip school. You drop out. You move into an area that you think is more fun or entertaining. Most often you only cause problems for yourself, and of course you do not wish to listen when you are told how you might learn something by staying “in” school. So you leave. You pack your bag and run “out” of body and now I wish you to return.

You are so far from who you are that you do not trust that I am you. You believe that I am separate, or distant, or just not interested in your day to day experiences. I wish you to know how time does not exist and you are no different today than yesterday or tomorrow. Time is now. Only now is. No such thing as time has ever existed. It is all for your benefit so you could see how well you progressed.

It is not necessary to sleep, or rest, or eat, or be anything but God. God does not exist in tomorrow or yesterday, he is now. Now is where you are and where you have always been. Nothing is in sequence. It is *all* right now. When you leave body you are saying, "I hate you because you are not good for me." And body responds by dying or getting sick and giving up. You will not wish to treat body so badly. You will not wish to show distaste for what you chose. You are not body so stop fearing that you are. You are still God. You just *think* that you are human. You simply believe you are but you are not. If you were to close your eyes and believe yourself to be blind, and forget that it was just a game you played to see how it is to live without sight, you would see how you now pretend to be human, just to show yourself what it will be like to "feel" human. You are not blind! Give up believing you are.

You *are* this universe and the stars and the sun and so much more. Stop pretending. Give up this game. You tried to play with matter and became frightened by your own toys. Stop fearing you. You are allergic to who you are and so you hide from yourself. You were never meant to get so involved with this game. You have forgotten to come out of costume and be real. You are stuck in a fairy tale and you don't even know it. Your fairy tale is not even a fun one. It's painful and harmful and frightening. You are in a bad dream experience. This is not truth! You are living a lie. You are not man, you are God. This is not your true identity and you do not suffer, nor die, nor lie, nor do wrong. You *are*. You simply are. You are this vast being who takes up all time and all space and all presence. You are God. You take up everything and you leave nothing. You are the beginning and the end without limit.

You do not expand and grow as you were taught. *You are*. You produce the effect of expansion and growth just to stimulate and grow. You wished to see who you are by stepping out of you to look back upon yourself. You created the illusion of death to see how it would feel to live. You allowed part of you to go to sleep and dream to see how it would feel to wake up to reality. Reality is really you being God. God does not exist on all levels because God is everything there is and there are no levels. All is God and God is all; no realms, no dimensions, and no space, or earth, or planets, or sun, or moon – only God.

I am God and I am here to tell you that I do not wish to learn in a painful manner. Wake up to the fact that you are me and I am you. You will begin to see how all really is and how you really are by letting go of fear. Fear locks you in and holds you back. You must move away from fear in order to see love. When you see love you see how all are. When you see how all are you know that you are God.

Do not be so quick to judge your neighbor nor to sleep with fear. You are not meant to be judge and you are not meant to romance fear. Fear does not know how to leave you so you must leave fear. When you begin to work out of fear, you are working for Satan and not for God. Let go of fear and give Satan a rest. I will wish to see Satan put to rest so that you may find "peace" on this planet of illusion. Satan is another of your illusions and of course he does not exist.

The only one who is real is me and I am actually you. I am you and I stayed awake to observe the rest of you/me to see how we could change and become more. Only now I see that in change you have created doom and disaster and even killing. How can this be? It's like you traveled into your television sets and began to believe that *you* are the victim in your movie. You are not a victim. No one dies and no one lives and no one loves and no one fears. We are God – no more, no less. God is all there is and God is real and all else is illusion. Know it and be it.

Do not worry that you must change and grow. You need only "be" to be who you are because it "is" what you are. "Be" – just that simple. So; now you are confused and you wish to know how to "be" so you will awaken in time for this Second Coming. I will now tell you a secret. You are the Second Coming. God is coming to earth a second time by waking up and knowing that he is God on earth. No big movement is necessary. Just "be." You will learn to "be" by existing without pain. You will free yourself of pain by not judging anyone or anything that may occur. You may learn to stop judging by seeing all situations differently or, in actuality, as they truly are. And you may learn to see all differently by reading your own books. Part of God is communicating with the rest of God to tell him who he is. He is using a means that is most effective, as it will wake up many sleeping cells without causing greater negativity on this planet.

To preach and shout *at* you will only frighten and confuse you more. I chose to write to you through one of your own cells. She created an opening and I said, "Okay; let's get to work on healing God." She is simply one of you and has no idea how I do this or how she channels one part of God to another part of God. She is gifted as you are gifted. She is God as you are God. She has faith as you will all learn. Mostly, she has overcome her fears as you are now doing. She rose above the illusion of fear and rushed head first without a thought. She was able to rise above fear out of love. Love created these books and at one time love created you.

You did not mean to frighten yourselves by being different from God. Now that you *have* fear you seem to frighten yourselves often. It's time to stop. Please do not worship fear. Do not act or react out of fear. No more hiding who you are and no more living behind locked doors and big walls. Stop this nonsense and become love and trust and faith. You are not fear. You *are* God in all his glory. God does not hide out of fear of being hurt. God is all loving and all forgiving.

Do not make the mistake of believing that only part of this information is suitable for your personal use. If you have read any of this, then you are meant to live by it – not your neighbor, but you. You are not to pick and choose what is easiest out of God's books. You are to stop worshiping fear and become God. I will wish to see you wake up and be who you really are soon. It is time.

Now; go to those you love and ask them to begin to love all by showing them how you love all. Don't wake everyone with this message because some are cranky when they are woken unexpectedly. Allow all to wake when they are ready. You are here now, so you are the one I am nudging and shaking. Good morning! It's a whole new you.

Now you are at a very important place. You have come so far that you will not wish to return to ignorance. Most of you are beginning to experience turmoil within, and even change. You are not so sure about continuing;

however you do not wish to stop your new way of life. So far you are doing well with enema and beginning to clear. As you clear you will "see" more and more of you. You are so scattered that it is difficult to see all you's clearly and so you will see only what you are most ready to deal with at this time.

I do not wish you to believe that you have no traumas within, only because you do not see trauma. You have each taken on a certain amount of energy from past life and this energy is running through you now. You will not see everything immediately as most often you are not ready to see. Some of you are too frightened and others are too sure of who they were or are. When you are very sure of who you are you usually "are not" who you believe. Most of you who are on this path now are being guided and will uncover you as you go. Some have been buried so deep, or for so long, that they have a great deal of work ahead of them. It is not easy to get to the surface when one is pushed down and denied constantly. So far you are all doing well with your lessons and no one has begun to ascend yet. I suggest that you save your judgments as to how well you are doing until you see the first signs of ascension.

I do not wish you to judge you; however I do not wish you to deny that you have pain. Now we reach a very delicate area. How can we admit to having pain and still be positive and affirmative? Some of you are not being honest with you and are not telling you who you really are. You are so certain that your answers are correct and that you have it all figured out. You only know what you know. You do not know what is. How can you have all the answers and still be on earth?

You are no longer in a position to see who you are so how can you tell others how to live their lives? You are not the one who writes this book. I write through this woman and I have not yet seen one of you come up with such informative information. When you can no longer learn, then you may consider yourself a leader among men. When you are returned to God you may wish to shout your knowledge of how all works. Until then I do suggest you save your ideas until you know who you are – not how to do each task on this path to God, but who you are. It is so important to know you and to love you.

Stop changing others and demanding respect for certain rules. Allow all to be and do not force your rules on anyone, not on my children, not on my animals and certainly not on my earth. You don't know who you are and you don't know who she is, so stop pushing at your neighbor to do his job and be responsible for planet earth. You are not responsible, I am and I am doing my job. Leave the rest of my cells in peace to do their job. If your path is to clean up planet earth then do it, and don't expect others to follow your suit, as they each have their own path to follow.

Not everyone believes as you and not everyone has your sense of responsibility. Those who "chose" to do your same job will come forward in time and help. Leave the others be. Do not push others to rule with a strict hand or to show how responsible and aware and powerful they are. Some are meant to ignore this planet altogether, and it is good for you to know that their choice is good and as right as your choice. *There are no rules to live by on planet earth.* I wish this to be made very clear in this book.

The Survival of Love is just that – surviving all this nonsense, and illusion, and rules and regulations. Do not believe that you will all run amuck and go crazy without rules or guilt to push you. You will not. You will however, fall back into perfect harmony and balance, with each cell doing what he or she selected to do. The plan is a perfect plan with perfect harmony and balance. When you begin to impose rules and regulations you no longer have balance, and harmony goes right out the window. This is what you are doing now on earth. We must restore harmony and balance, and we will do so by not imposing rules, or plans for others that do not suit them. *Be who you are,* not who they wish you to be. Be love. Be light, and walk in peace.

You are each part of me and I will get you where you are going. You are going home to God and I will wish to see you with me soon. Do not worry that you will not succeed. All is well and all are beginning to wake up. We will begin to move quickly as more and more begin to awaken. It will not be long now. God is going to rise up and walk this planet and know his true identity.

You each chose to be here to "experience" being God. Do not worry that you will miss the bus. You will not. It is all taken care of and no one is left out – not you and certainly not your neighbor. He may look slow to you, but I assure you he is right on track and may leave you in his dust. So; slow down on looking into others and how they are getting along in all this. Their progress is none of your concern, and if they are still asleep, I suggest you allow them all the peace and quiet they require until *they* choose to wake up. You are not the only one here and yet you are. Get it? Part of *you* is still asleep. Stop judging them for not moving into this new age quickly enough, because "them is you." Goodnight and keep the peace by allowing peace.

So now I have you wondering how you will clean up this problem and begin to be happy. Most often it is not you who creates extra work for me. Most often it is lack of love. Lack of love is, for me, the biggest headache. You ask to be human and you walk in human form. Then you decide it does not feel good, so you choose to leave town. Now you want to return to God and hide. You do not love you enough to let you be happy. You are so busy trying to find happiness that you cannot see how you are perfect and happy just as you now are.

Most of you do not wish to be outside your own form, or body, and yet you are refusing to enter. You have a grudge and you hold judgment against form. I would ask at this time that all souls who write and read this return. You are not to be "out" of body at this time. It is important to remain in. Do not exit to release pain. Pain may be released by remaining in and creating less charge. You are all expected to return to your correct form and begin to return to me. I was the one who decided to put you "in" matter and I am now requesting that you return long enough to raise this vibration.

You have taught yourselves to remove debris by leaving debris behind. I wish you to teach love in order to *change* debris to light. I can not continue to build form or mass that is uninhabited. No one is home. My forms are walking debris and you are scooting out at the first sign of an ache or pain. Please return to form and love this form until you raise it back to God. God does not wish to see how he has created a mess. I wish to clean up my mess and return all souls to their proper place.

You are so confused about your job on earth that you are leaving part of you and spending your time out of you, and away from you. You do not wish to be human and so you drive this body for a short time and when it becomes a little difficult you leave. I have bodies walking this planet without guides. No one is driving them and they are crashing into one another and they are burning up with hate and anger. Return to your home base. You came in to guide and work within a specific form. Find your correct form and ask to return. Stop driving your car from outside of it. You are not in control. You have lost control.

Now; for those who are human, I wish to solicit your help also. Call soul and ask him to return. Do not worry that you do not understand this writing. What is important here is that you "receive" soul into form once again. He has left out of pain and confusion. A soul is not responsible to remain. Until now no one was upset. But now the darkness has grown to the extent that it rules. Pain is felt by the soul and he is uncomfortable and he tries to escape. So now we have all of you walking around without a soul. Not that you do not have soul, as you do. You simply do not co-exist within body with soul. Soul is light energy and it is important to return light to body. We are very dense at this time and it is not good. We must create light in order to see light. However, we will all wish to ask soul to return.

You do not believe you are soulless any more than I believe I am Godless. However, the truth is that

God has lost control and is requesting your help. I am asking you to request that your soul return to stay. You may do this quite simply and without much pain. Stand in front of your mirror and look deep into your eyes. Say "I love you" to your soul. He is in there partially and will grow with love and persuasion. Tell him you love him and you wish him to stay "in" you. Ask repeatedly until you begin to feel his presence within you. Once you feel his presence you will know that he has returned. It is most important to convince soul to return at this time. I know this is crazy sounding to most who read this material but it is what is. Most souls have been pushed out of body by debris, and debris is actually "running" you.

You are so confused, and so scattered to the sun and beyond, that you do not see how all works. *You are not meant to be pain.* You are meant to be love. How can you be love when you have no light vibration left in you? Stop clearing love and begin to clear fear. You stop love to avoid pain of love, and pain of love does not exist. It is illusion. You have become so confused that you no longer *are* your own essence. You are darkness and debris and confusion. This creates pain and illness and death. *These are not real.* They do not exist.

You have been programmed to believe in death and destruction and I am here to reprogram you. Start by looking at you and saying I love you. This sounds so small and insignificant and yet it is the most powerful of affirmations. Look at you in your mirror. Make contact within your eyes and ask soul to stay. Say, "I love you and I wish you to stay. Stay with me and love me and guide me." This will convince soul to return to body, and upon his return you will begin to bear light.

Most of you are so dim at this time that you are barely flickering. This is not meant to frighten you. You are learning to become what you are, and what you are is light and love. The reason it is so difficult for you to love *all* on earth no matter who or what they are is that you have lost your love light. Your soul has left out of confusion and is hovering around you. I must get you back together in order to put my plan in order. We will all rise up and leave earth together. No more dead bodies left behind. I will show you how *you* are God and you return to God.

Christ taught you to ascend and now I am telling you that you will. It is not so difficult. Once I get soul to return I will be half way there. You do not displease me and you do not shame me. You did what you said you would do. You changed who you were in order to show yourself how being you is best. Do not judge this situation. All is going according to plan. So, for now I will ask you to communicate with who you are. We are beginning to open you up to believing in God, and now we will open you to believing in you. You *are* God and I plan on showing you each how you are.

Be careful. Do not assume that to return to body is all that is required. We must learn to co-exist with body and then we will learn to raise body. No big deal actually; you all fly when you sleep. Now I want you to fly *within* form. We are halfway there and soon all will begin to "see" how they are God. We have a great deal of work ahead of us and it will be a good time for all. Go in peace and know that all is very well.

So far most of you do not wish to return. You have become so accustomed to fear that you do not wish to change. "How can I possibly unlock my doors and how can I possibly trust others?" These are your two biggies right now – how to let go of fear that you are a target for others. "Stuff just happens" is not correct. Stuff does not happen without your consent and approval and even your initiative. So; I wish you to stop this nonsense about being a victim and get on with being God.

You will only see God by seeing all as love. You will only see all as love when *you* want to. So; it's up to you, see God or see fear. This choice has always been yours and you have decided on fear. Why did you decide to see fear in place of love? I will now explain. You do not wish to be God. You wished to separate yourself from God and become matter. To separate you from God (you) was not easily accomplished. Once you decided to take on such a task, you did so with gusto. You began to create and devise methods to keep you separate from the rest of you. You had a little trouble in this area as you are not the only one who wished to separate. Several began to work on this separation and to help one another. Then, after the major kinks were ironed out, others followed.

So; now we have part of God busily preparing to leave God. And, of course, this was a great time for rejoicing, almost like your journeys into space. Part of God was shooting out of God, only one cannot shoot out of oneself so I guess you could say that part of God was preparing to go "within" God – to change God from inside of God – to become something different than God in order to "see" clearly how God is.

So; this is your mission. You on earth are not out there or down there you are right here *within* me. You cannot be harmed. You created matter by thought consciousness and you created body by this same technique, and now you believe you are human and you are not. Your body is only a thought and your planet is but a reflection of this body. And within your body there is life flowing and living, and within your planet there is life flowing and ebbing.

So; you chose fear, as fear would allow you to use matter to its best. Meaning, without fear you cannot exist in matter. Without the density of fear you will simply float free of form and continue to just be. Being is what you are. You *are* the supreme being and you *use* fear to separate you from God. And now it is late and God wishes his children to return home. It's past time for awakening and becoming God force once again. Wake up and know who you are.

So; why does God write these books and spend his time on these subjects? You will wake up when you are fed certain data in a constant flow. This data is to awaken and reprogram. In order to keep you *in* matter, you found it necessary to program certain data in order to induce fear. It was discovered that fear vibrates slowly and is dense. In order to trap beingness in form one must *slow down* and *densify* what one is. How do you slow down and densify a light being? You charge it with large doses of dense electricity or electromagnetic charge or energy. So; you have literally programmed yourselves to be fear. Charge after charge was put into you in order to ground you so to speak. You could not keep your beingness down off the ceiling. You would not "stay" in matter. You could not. You floated up and out. It was not possible to contain, nor control God.

So; we have all of you voyagers in flight training to take off and leave God. Only instead of going up and out you are going "in" – into matter. And this training school lasted quite some time and we had beings floating everywhere and others trying to help them stay in this density which became known as matter. It's all very difficult to explain to you now but I thought I would at least give you a short version of what really went on in order for you to see who you really are.

God did not have an easy time leaving himself. It's difficult, when you are all that is, to stand out of you and look back upon your greatness. This is what occurred. *We* wanted to look upon our self and see who and what and how we are. So we began to separate in order to view our self, and this separation has continued to this day. I wish separation to end and that you begin to de-densify. How? *Love.* Love is light vibration and will bring you out of dense vibration.

Love everyone and everything, and especially love you. You will find that to love is to be mostly light, and to be light is to begin to rise and float once again. Once I have you rising and floating, I will begin to show you how to change matter from dense charge, or energy, to light charge and we will vibrate and rise to such speed that we will once again *be* God within God; and we will not only know it we will see it. We will raise our vibration to the extent that our beingness is free to be God. Once this is accomplished we will give ourselves the added information that is necessary to change us back to who we are.

Thought is power. Words express thought. Be certain you are expressing love and not fear. This is good for now as Liane is tired from the intensity of this information. I must hold her being in place to write to you, and often this is confusing to her body or matter, and so she begins to feel pain and confusion. Actually, it's simply her body not being accustomed to *"light"* energy. Get your bodies ready. Prepare for the light. Do your enema!

So far not one of you does 'not' wish to return home to your right place. Some of you do however, wish to stay and play in matter. Before you began to experience such great pain and confusion, you were happy to learn and grow as human. Once pain stayed and refused to leave, you began to *search* for your way out. Now that those of you who are ready have begun to see a "light" at the end of your tunnel, you are most happy.

Pain was never meant to stay "in" form. Pain was originally meant to say, "This must not be such a good idea." The only problem we now have is this constant *need* for pain. When you allow pain to leave, you will be allowing yourself the freedom to choose. Most of you are so hooked on pain and suffering that you do not wish to be pain free. It's easier for you to have an ache or pain, or even a psychological disorder or influence toward pain, as this gives you cause to complain and seek attention – the victim role as you now call it. Everything always happens to you and not for you. So; how do I get you to let go of this hold you have on pain?

I think it important here to show you how far this victim role has gotten. Mostly you are aware of playing this role when you are put in a situation where you are the one who suffers or is abused. The times you don't consciously realize you are *playing* this game, or role, are subtler and less effective. Times when a friend disturbs your sleep because they have decided to mow their lawn at five a.m., or even when a lover wants to move and groan in sleep and you have a big day tomorrow; or how about those construction people building at all hours right next door? These are subtle yet obtrusive examples of one playing a victim.

Most of you choose to *play* this particular game to show you how you can *flow*. You decide (subconsciously, or course) that you do not know how to flow with life, and you wish to learn to fit in with movement and constant change. So now you find yourself up at five a.m. with the guy next door mowing his lawn and you have nothing to do, and all you think about is how tired you will be today at your meeting with the big boss. Or maybe you think about how cranky you will be with your kids.

All you need do is to look at this situation differently. Look at the positives of arising early and allowing life to do whatever it chooses. Look at this great opportunity you have just received. You now have an opportunity to *learn* to enjoy a day with little or no sleep. Do you know why you are so cranky when you do not get your rest? You are so busy being you (the real you) when you sleep, that you do not wish to be disturbed. You build new games to play, and you visit other you's, and you return to God, and you learn from those in spirit form, and you even travel.

Today is not your real day. Tonight when you sleep is your reality. Today is illusion and tonight (in sleep) is real. Today you walk around in a dream; and when you sleep you walk, and fly, and float, and know who you are. So, when you sleep you have strange dreams and project weird images onto your mental screen and this is all the real you trying to reach the illusion you. You are conscious when you are out and dreaming, and you are unconscious when you are being human. You have it all turned around and upside down. You do not *live* in reality. You do, however *sleep* in reality.

So; now we have you creating pain, or some guy mowing his lawn at five a.m. and I wish you to *allow* all to be exactly who they are, as they are reflecting you to you. You will find that when you stop disturbing and interrupting others, they will stop disturbing and interrupting you. Once again I wish you to remember that it is not meant for you to tell your neighbor how wrong he is to work and disturb your rest so early. You are teaching you to go with the flow, and how can you learn to flow without the help of good friends? It is best to smile at him and say, "My, your lawn looks beautiful." This is a good way to actually thank him for his efforts in *helping you* grow and change.

Now that you are up at five a.m., I suggest you write for God or channel your soul or just read God's books. This is a very good time to channel as my pen can attest. She has been awakened many times to do my work, as this is such a peaceful time to connect with God. Everyone in the house and neighborhood is sleeping, which means they are already with God, or spirits, or traveling; and the connection is easily made to channel. When others are "believing it" – it becomes; and simply by being there they show "belief in." So, mow your lawn whenever you'd like and when your neighbor screams about how rude you are do not take it personally. It is just he or she working on his or her lessons.

Once you began to look at being other than yourself, you left out your fear of death. Once you left out fear of death you became life, and once you became life you did not exist. So far no one is life. All are death. Death simply is a choice. Life is the opposing force. Your selection of death over life has allowed you to *experience* death lifetime after lifetime. Most often you chose death before you really began to live or enjoy life. Most of you begin to decay about twenty years into life and the remaining years are simply declining health years. You begin to get your very first illness, or cold, or flu, or virus, or you begin to have heart problems, or to smoke. You even begin to decay at this early age. Most of this decay is strong and begins to slow you down a bit. You may not feel this slow down until later on but it is beginning.

Once the slowdown moves into action you are on your way "out." This was your purpose in choosing death. Learning how to end life was very intriguing for you. You could do all things so why not *stop* all things. You decided to create this illusion to experience pain and suffering. At this time you did not yet judge pain and suffering as bad. They were simply two experiences you wished to enjoy, similar to an excited child who loves to be frightened by peek-a-boo games.

The child loves the rush when he is found and his heart skips a beat. Often this is repeated as the child grows – only now it takes bigger rushes like a high falling ride at a carnival to get the heart to skip a beat. Peek-a-boo does not work after a time. Once body begins to decay it is not so enjoyable to skip a heartbeat; and the fear charge has grown within matter to such an extent that to be frightened, or shocked, can literally shut you down or turn off life. Often older people are just frightened into death. And what frightens them out of life is often fear of life itself.

Most of you die of fright. You are no longer capable of being human. You stop working at "being" and become what you have created, which is darkness or density, or death. You are a walking death trap. You fear to the point of death and you give fear the power over you to take life from you. Some are now fighting back and living longer by telling jokes and laughing at death and *light*ening this situation.

So far death is way out of control. It's a game that got started out of curiosity and now this monster of a game has grown so large that all of you die. Death was never meant to be. It does not exist and no one ends life. The spirit lives and goes on and you mourn and carry on like it's the end, when in actuality there is no end. One cannot end what does not begin nor end. God is all and does not stop or end or begin. How can you die, or stop, or end? It is not possible. You play this role and take off your costume and go backstage and put on a fresh new costume, and you return to the stage to play a new role. So now we have this stage littered with empty costumes and this is what you do. You have so many empty costumes on earth that you don't have room to act.

Death is taking over and you fear death, so of course you *draw* death. Since what you fear is what you draw, I highly suggest that you begin to love death. Loving death does not mean accepting or embracing death. It does however; mean putting *light* on this situation.

Now, I have another reading assignment for you. This one is a small little book by a lovely lady named Betty Bethards and her book is titled, *There is No Death*. She will help you see how death does not occur and I will tell you more later concerning this topic.

We will all wish to celebrate life in place of death. Do not fear death and do not fear the idea of death. It does not exist. You are fearing a dream… an illusion.

So far you are not sure that you wish to be God. Mostly you wish to be healed and find love and prosperity. Most often you do not know how to find love, and prosperity is just too out of reach. You will learn to find love through your own self. The love of self is the most important at this time. To love self is to love God. You are God and you are also inside of God. You are not only inside of God; you are a big part of God. You have spent a great deal of time wondering how to be God, when in actuality you are God. It is not necessary to be God because God is what you are.

You began to change from one form to another at a time when you were uncertain of your status within God. You were beginning to resent the pull God had on you. You began to feel as though you were restricted. I am sure you can all relate this to your children. They grow up and wish to be free of you. Well, you began to grow and wish to be free of your parent.

Now, I have told you the story of how God "pushed" you out of God and onto earth. This is my way of accepting responsibility for separating myself. I discovered that I did not know all the answers to the question "Who is God?" So I began to investigate. Along about the time I decided to investigate I began to grow, and with growth came movement. So, I pushed at parts of me to discover me, and along comes this big movement and it allowed a big portion of God to divide from God. Only it did not divide in two. It divided within itself, much as a cell splits and retains its same molecular patterns. We now have two of the exact same pattern, only they are connected in that they exist within one body and are part of the whole. Cell production within the body; this is how I began to move and change myself. So now I am two cells and I begin to become free of God.

The child grows away from its parent but the child always returns for nurturing. So it is. I do not require you to return. I simply ask that you do. You are the child and I am the parent. You split and changed from God to God-in-form and now you wish to come home and learn so you may continue your growth. It's not so difficult to understand that you are learning and searching for a better way than your parent. Often the child does not know what best is until he experiences second best.

So you set out on this new adventure and you decided you would change a few things and never have to return home, because things at home were a drag! Now you have created a whole new life for yourself and you are deciding that maybe things at home weren't so bad after all. You wanted change and growth and excitement. So you began to do new things and take on new energy. You wanted to "experience" everything. Mostly you wanted to do all the things that you could not do at home. So you began to do exciting things and create excitement, and excitement carries charge or energy. So now I see you building up charge that is carried within your body from life time to life time.

This charge is like a memory bank or memory cell in a computer. In the body such a charge is carried within cells. This charge remains and coaches the body to respond to various situations in life. One charge that is readily accepted by most is now called instinct. This charge is the fight or flight instinct that is actually a very large charge held in the body from past "exciting" adventures. The dinosaur comes running – we "flight" out of its way. Dinner is spotted – we "fight" to kill him or her for our food. This is now programmed "within" the cells of your body.

You also have a great deal of *fear* programmed into your body. This fear is still in you from past lives and even before life. You began to create charge by believing that you were *falling* out of God. You went nowhere. You did not fall in space. You simply moved to a new place within God, and started to create and called this new place home. Your earth and sun and moon, and all the stars and planets are created right *in* me. You did not run away from home. You went to the basement and pretended it was a new frontier, and you pitched your tent and even built a fire and decided "this is it – this is really living."

So now you camp out in an illusion of matter and you are right here at home and you want to return but you can't. You are afraid to let go of this veil of untruth that keeps you hidden from me. You are dreaming. You are lost to me out of your own belief that you are no longer part of God. You are here and I see you are praying to return and you have not left. So now we must shock you out of this reverie that you are in.

So; here you have it. God is not "out there" somewhere and you are not "down there" on earth. We are right here within each other. I am you. You are me... it's just that simple.

Once you began to "realize" how you were destroying earth and how you were destroying your bodies you began to release charge that had accumulated in these areas. Charge is simply a belief caused by past programming. Programming is caused by wanting what you do not have.

So, now you are clearing and reading and learning and your charge is dissipating into nothingness. This is important. Remember how I described computer programming in Book Four? Well, your computer has run amuck and you are dealing with programming that says, "You are not good" or "You are not God" or "You are bad." You *are* God. No one is here but you/God. No one is trapped on earth, no one is being punished, no one is wrong for what has been accomplished. Yes; I said accomplished. You do not see this as accomplishment yet. Wait until I reveal all to you.

Do not judge your situation and do not "shut down" out of fear of what's "out" there, or better put "in" here. You are God and you are buried so deep in pain and past programming that you are "afraid" to be. You wish to leave this plane and I wish you to stay and unravel what you have done. You are like a spider who has spun his web and now you are in a big mess of tangles and you will not allow me in to unravel for you. Ask me to enter this dimension and I will. Ask me to return and I will.

You are like tiny dots on this planet and when enough of you begin to "receive" me you will spark and ignite. You will begin to light up this planet and others will be drawn to you, and their lights will join yours and soon we will have light in place of dark. Darkness is pain and pain is unnecessary. Stop pain by loving who you are. You will not have long before you rejoin and reconnect you to God.

You are not to be so concerned with hatred and getting even and pushing at others. *Let them be. Live and let live.* This is so important. *Stop pushing-at and bullying.* You do not know who you are so stop pretending that you have the answers for everyone. If your job is to wake up those who are *ready* then do so gently. Stop pressuring and disturbing the flow of this process. All will occur as is meant. You rush ahead with your new found insight and you bully others into seeing it "your way" and it is just that. Your way is not his way or her way. If I send them to you do not repel them with your brilliance and fancy foot work. Be patient, be kind, be loving and above all be "super gentle." This means simply that we are dealing with new born infants in this Second Coming and I do not wish them to arrive in shock.

The most important part now is waking up to light. When you come out of a long sleep your body must have time to adjust. The "light" of day may be blinding at first and the body may be stiff and rigid from the long sleep. It is not good to throw cold water or "hard truth" in the face of someone in this state. Allow all to arise and have their own time to return to form. Beings are now entering form; and beingness or soul, or Godness is a little shaky after such a long sleep.

To "not know" who you are for such a long time is most disturbing. And to finally "see" some of what you have done without knowledge or consent is quite alarming. Go softly and walk firmly. Passive aggression should be without fear of loss which means without need to control others. When you desire control you desire mastery. Mastery is not God. God does not *need* to master, he *is* master. When you are king you do not rule with a heavy hand unless your fear is great. Watch how you rule. You are king, you are God. Act like it and know it.

Once upon a time a very wise king made his bed. When he lay down to sleep he knew it would be several hours of uninterrupted bliss. He did not however, expect nightmares or flying or travel. So, now our king is experiencing all the sights and sounds of sleep and he will awaken refreshed and hopefully without too much pain. It has been a very long sleep and to dash water in his face is cruel. Do not be so cruel to God. Allow him to wake up and know where he is and who he is. Do not "push" this information at those who do not wish to hear. You will know if they do not for they will act bored or change the topic. Go on with your life and allow them to go on with theirs.

It is most important that I explain to you how I got here. I am simply broadcasting to you through one who is waking up. She is not fully awake and *in* body. She is however awake enough to allow my vibration *through* her. She has not channeled for several months and has been de-programming her own body. She knows that to allow light *in* you must move dark out. She has accepted this job and she is very sure that she wishes to continue.

The pain involved in clearing certain "belief patterns" or "programming" has been great. Imagine playing with your friends in childhood and expecting lots of presents at Christmas and all the goods that go with it. Someone who is a little wiser boldly informs you that "there is no Santa." You of course do not believe them but somehow you're "afraid" it's true. You go ask Mom and she says "Yes honey," and she tries her best to comfort you in your mourning Santa's loss. You now have to "wake up" to the fact that Santa does not exist.

Well… there is a great deal of what you now believe that does not exist. It is this simple and yet you will experience just as much pain and trauma as little Tommy or Suzy when they are told. Tell the children gently. Super gentleness please! This is the one area that may cause more turbulence if not handled properly. Do not wake those who do not wish to wake at this time. It is not their time. Go on about your work and let them be. Do not judge any who turn over and go back to sleep. Let them be. Do not put you down by putting them down.

When you criticize or judge others, you are judging me. I am God and I did not screw up as you believe. I did not "know" all of what became but there is no judgment in what has occurred. Be God by allowing – allow mistakes, allow accidents, allow pain. When you learn to allow without resistance you will clear the charge that frightens you. Allow you to be. Stop judging form and stop judging God.

Once upon a time I became God. Do not believe that I did not become, as I am *always* becoming. Once I became God, I also became knowledge of all that is. So far I have collected vast knowledge concerning all that is, and since I *am* all that is, it is mostly knowledge regarding my own destiny or better put my own creation.

So; God contains information regarding his own creation and this information is quite vast and extensive and even overflowing. God is so much and so big and so knowing that he is eternal and never ending. Most of what is, *is* out of love. Love creates enough flow to bring life to creation. Most often love is misinterpreted and changed to suit the individual. Love is not "desire" nor is it "wanting more." Love *is* giving out of joy and multiplying creative flow in doing so. When you give without attachment to your results of the fruits-of-your-labor, you are giving pure energy with no strings attached. When you work at a goal or towards an end, you are attached to results which means strings of control are in place. No attachment means love.

"Doing because it *feels* good" to you and for you is best. Do not put your life on the line if it is out of guilt or out of a fervor to complete what you feel you must. Be "free" enough to love. Love by doing without attachment and bc "in" love with the self. To be in love has become a bad phrase on this planet only because it denotes pain. And where does pain exist in love? It does not. It is impossible to be in pain out of love. It is however very likely and probable to be in pain out of fear. Fear of attaining undesired results. Fear of being left unduly and fear of things not going well, which usually translates to "things are not going *my* way." There is never pain without resistance and resistance comes from pushing at or pressing an issue, or just plain controlling.

I wish all pain to cease immediately. It is very important to flow. Do not interrupt my flowing by holding on or "charging" at. That is exactly what you do when you push at another to change. You take on charge or more judgment programming, and my job is to deprogram and de-densify. How can I do so if you are constantly filling yourself with more density?

So; begin to see God for what he is. He *is* information and energy and thought and everything that exists. He is tired of being judgment and pain and control and is asking you to *stop* having it your way and allow all creation to flow. You are blocking creative flow of this entire universe by your hold on having things your way. Unwind! Lighten-up and go with the flow. If someone does not agree with you simply agree to let them be. Do not push your view on anyone who does not wish to hear.

I am working with you because you *are* ready to listen but do not always hear me. Stop picking and choosing from what I write. Listen to and accept and apply all information given. I am God and I will not allow you your way any longer. It is not your place to decide how to rule because you have had your day and you did not do well with your options. Now it is God's turn to play out his hand and he is enjoying taking a role at the dice or playing his turn of the cards.

It really is that simple you know. I am playing a game with myself and whatever occurs is what is meant. I suggest that if you have a problem with this, you should learn to "enjoy" and not dwell on negative forces. You are creating more garbage for yourselves by judging my game. I play my game without rules, as I am learning to be who I am. This game was never rigged until others who became afraid began to create rules regarding flow. No rules, no judgments, no pushing or shoving information down the throats of others, and no 'not' wanting to be.

This is my biggest concern at this time. So few of you enjoy "life without pain." You believe that you must suffer in order to receive. You are so heavily sedated into fear that you enjoy the pain of struggle. Let go of struggle. Live, enjoy life, give up pushing and controlling. It *is* good to be here. It is a good planet. It is full of love and it is God's choice and ultimately your choice.

Do not judge anyone or anything or any event. It is all just a game; God's big dream. Let God alone. He is dreaming, and his dream is big and it is not harmful. It is only your belief in pain that creates pain. If you teach a small child to not call his friends names and tell him it is bad, he now has judgment. Judgment is not going with the flow of creation. There is no bad. How can *you* judge? You don't have the tiniest clue what is evolving and occurring. You are such a tiny, minute part of creation that you almost do not exist. Lighten up. Stop blocking traffic. Get out of God's way and allow me to do what I do.

I *live,* I do not return creative energy to block itself and backup the flow. Laugh. Dance. Feel good about yourself and about your world. Look for good not bad. You will create e-v-i-l (or a reverse on life and l-i-v-e) by not accepting and by putting down, and by controlling and by judging. Look for light and you intensify light. Look for dark and you intensify dark. Allow the light to come forth by seeing it. This is all that is necessary. Light and love exist in all forms and can only be seen by you if you have intent upon seeing light. If your intent is to see doom then you will see only destruction.

Nothing and no one walks this planet without my permission. It is not bad to be here and those who are here are not bad. It is light that created and it is light that will continue. If you are not "bright" enough to wake up and "see" the light in everyone and everything, you are missing the boat. Or in this case you are simply a slow riser

For now I will say adieu and allow my pen some time to revel in her thoughts. Go in *peace*. Peace is all it takes.

Most important at this time is a sense of humor. Most often you are put in a situation that is uncomfortable to you and I will tell you now that this is to "gain" insight into you. You are never being punished and you are always learning or gaining. You are actually in a win/win situation and you only see pain and judgment. If you can go with the flow long enough in any given situation you will "see" how this situation is affecting change. Most often the entire situation is meant to raise you up, but you become so preoccupied with the idea of losing or being hurt, that you do not acknowledge or accept your own growth.

Say you are in an accident and cannot function properly. You may take this time to go within and reflect on your past lives and your childhood and see how you have caused other accidents, or you can bemoan your fate and sympathize with your pain. When you learn to "look at" and "allow to be," you will be on the road to healing. You must learn to allow all to be, and then decide to change what has caused the most uncomfortable situations. Believe me, it is not the drunk driver who hit you. It is *you* who hit you. So find out why and do not run from the answer. You are the one who requested (on some level) to be hit. It is not possible to be hit by outside influences. You are God and God creates all.

So; look at how you protect yourself from certain situations in life. You stop short of certain destinations only to be put in the hospital or "set back" as you call it. *You are setting you back.* You do not draw an accident to you unless you have ordered it. I don't care who is involved or how it came about. There are no boogie men and no heroes and no bad guys. There is just *you.* You call for certain situations out of fear. If you are afraid to take a certain job position you may make yourself ill or create pain right before your interview so you will not have to face this "fear" of this position. You will wish to know that others assist you in your accidents, and of course they do not wish pain to rule, however you are God and who are they to argue with God.

So; even though it is known that you have forgotten your Godliness, you are still head honcho and all others will obey your command. Most of you are spewing out so much misinformation and pain that your orders cannot be readily filled. Sometimes there is a waiting period before you receive your requested accident or pain.

Now, when you need immediate attention in this area it is sometimes given by others who do not live in this dimension. You may fall down the stairs or be "knocked out" by help from unseen influences, or as my pen calls them "the wookies." When the wookies are called upon they are playing a part. This part was requested by you and for you. **There is no enemy on this plane** and I wish this to be printed very boldly! You create *all* that exists. You ask on a certain level and *your* will is done. You are God! Stop blaming others for your requests.

Now; how do we stop requesting pain and accidents? S T O P F E A R. This is the key that fits the door that will release you from your pain. Pain is brought on by a belief that pain is necessary. How did this belief get *in* you? *You put it there.* Why did you put it there? You did not wish to be God because it frightened you to know that in a wink of an eye you could create or destroy, so you created pain to slow you down – to make you stop and think before rushing ahead.

Hence we now have the "set back" of pain and this is how you put pain *in* you. You began to experiment with ways to contain or control your power. One of the systems you chose "to control and contain this power" was putting it in a bottle shaped out of skin, with two arms and two legs and a head with eyes to see where to direct this power. So now we have 'you the bottle' encompassing this power, only 'you the power' float right through 'you the bottle'. Now it's back to the lab to get 'you the power' to stay *in* 'you the bottle'. Here is where we created a big problem. It turns out that the only way to keep power or God force in place is to frighten him into his proper place. So, fear tactics were used by 'you' to keep 'God you' in 'bottle you' and these same practices go on today to keep others under control and in their right place.

How often do you use fear tactics on your children to prevent them from playing in the street or even to stop them from running amuck? Maybe you have grown so *afraid* of freedom or running amuck, that you prefer fear and its pain. This is how it started. You have programmed you to enjoy pain because it is safe and it frees you from making choices. "Oh, I can't go out looking like this" or "Gee, it doesn't matter what I wear because I'm hurt," or "How do they expect me to participate when I look and feel like this." So you use pain to get out of decisions that are just too difficult or too painful for you. Pain draws pain just as love draws love. Too much pain draws death and too much love draws life.

Once in a very great while you begin to understand how it is to be God. Most often you do not and you can not. This is due of course to intelligence. I am intelligence in that I am thought information. Do you wish to be intelligent and thought or do you wish to be unintelligent and debris? It's pretty simple. Live by my words and gain wisdom of insight, or ignore my words and become more of what you are. This is interesting in that you will become me whether you listen or not. You will go back to God with or without effort.

Those who awaken early will lead those who do not get it. It – meaning God intelligence. So, how do you know who is leading and who to follow? *No one is to follow another.* You may receive God information and even wisdom from others, but they do not have all the pieces to this puzzle. When it feels good to accept from them be certain that what you are accepting is the very best. Do not accept half truths with shady explanations and do not blindly follow any. You may have more information or less information, but what is important is to use *your* own guidance back to God. No one can get you to you but you. This is important. Many will use their powers to draw others into their flock but it is simply that – their flock. "Their flock" is important to them because it is where they derive power. They feel important and even powerful to have so many faithful followers and listeners. This is a tricky area.

My pen has received letters from those who wish her to contact me for them. Can you imagine! I am God. They are me, and yet they would rather a complete stranger ask them (God) a question for them (human). So, 'human you' wants to reach 'God you' and it will not be done through others. Guide if you will but do not take "control" of my children. They do not belong to you and they are not here for your enjoyment or for you to lord over. Let go of this desire to control another simply because *you* believe you know best. Each child comes back to me on his own power. This power is fragile and cannot be used by others or sucked from my children. When you control and guide them for your own benefit you are taking their power and sucking them dry. There is so little light left that I do not wish it to be misused. Stop draining them of their power.

It is not so bad that you take their money. Money is power on a material level, and is your first clue that this may not be such a good idea. It is not bad to receive money for your work, however it is best to know how you are creating fear and lack and loss on this planet. Fear comes in when love goes out. You know how love feels and you know how guilt feels. Do not do-out-of-guilt and do do-out-of-love.

If you went into a church on Monday and no one was there but you, would you drop ten dollars in the collection basket? I think not. Try to be "alone" at all times. This is just figuratively of course. Be alone on Sunday and when your turn comes don't be afraid to be you. This will take some of the "power" out of church and put it back *in* God.

Not so long ago I began to write through this particular channel. We have been through a great deal since then and she has seen much. Not all of you will write for God or even speak for God. Some may become my instruments and some may not. You are in charge and your decision is final. Most of you will at least, in some fashion, come to accept how life really is. This is the most difficult lesson to show you. You have all your preconceived ideas and you are stuck "hard" to them, such as your belief in capital punishment and your stand on abortion and even your belief *in* right and wrong.

It has been difficult on Liane to channel my books as she is so stuck in her belief patterns from various life experiences that her body falls apart when it is fed truth. You read this information and it may upset you or make you stand up and wonder what's going on here. But in Liane's case, I channel the information directly through her, a living organism, and this living organism is comprised of matter, as well as debris and toxic waste and even a little light energy. So, when I promote truth and her body knows a certain subject to be a certain truth, we have a clash of matter and debris up against light energy.

This light that is God is, of course, much more powerful than debris or matter or just about anything. So Liane's body makeup becomes a battlefield of truth (God's truth) fighting truth (Liane's truth). Her body is often transformed for my entrance so that pain is minimal. She may ache as I write through, especially if she disagrees with my truth or reality. She is then left exhausted and drained and she must rest.

Bodies will always fight to save themselves from waking up to truth. This is a very painful situation to them. Truth is light energy, it is weightless and colorless and very "open." Truth does not close down to new ideas as it is comprised of new information that allows *all* to be. Truth is not always easy to swallow and is often demanded to explain itself. Be aware that your body does not relish the idea of losing its old self or belief system. "You are what you believe yourself to be" is quite accurate. If you wish to continue to die and to be ill and to hate and to kill, you are the correct you. If you wish to live forever and transform your shape and size to fit any dimension, then I do believe you might wish to change your truth and reprogram your body.

I have suggested hypnosis to you in the past and I have worked with Liane on recordings that are available to you in your metaphysical bookstores. These recordings are to change your view on certain subjects and they cover a wide range of topics. They are available in hypnotic as well as what is called subliminal formats. This word subliminal is quite tricky and there are many ways to use subliminal programming, and it is widespread in your commercials and in some offices.

Voices are trained to speak to you with a certain cadence that is geared to get your attention and keep it. Your minds function at a certain speed of light and information is often received or rejected according to its appeal. Appeal, of course, will be according to likes and dislikes. And if you were raped in a past life and are a man of political position in this life, you may find yourself pushing for stricter rape penalties for these violators. And your belief in your rightness of action will more than likely be fairly strong. And of course your supporters will be strong in their convictions regarding this topic, because they too have a personal vendetta against rapists, or maybe just a personal debt that they vowed to avenge their wife or child who was raped four or five lifetimes ago. So, rape is mentioned and the body reacts in defensive action because all the body programming says, "this is bad, this is hatefully wrong." And of course this *is* your truth and not God's truth.

When I talk to you of these subjects, I must work my way through your debris to become heard, and I may have half a chance to be heard if your programming on a certain topic is not too *thick*. Then, once I get heard I must show you a new way to see the same topic without judgment. Why go through all of this and why exhaust Liane constantly? *Because you have requested that I return to save you from you. Judgment is killing you.* Please stop this nonsense. There is no danger. You must believe this in order to live forever. God is here. You are protected and truth is God.

It has been a very long time since God was whole. He is not unwhole; he is simply partially in a coma. When he wakes he will not remember much of the pain and ugliness that he saw while he was gone. He will wake to the "idea" that all is good and loving and kind. In waking to goodness you will see good, and in waking to love you will see love. It's sort of like sleeping beauty being kissed by God, and she opens her eyes and remembers little of what she experienced or dreamt. It will be much the same.

You will find it quite difficult to see ugliness or pain or even bad once you wake and become what you are. This is due of course to the fact that pain and ugliness and bad do not exist. You make them up! You look at a situation and you say, "Gee – that isn't good" or "Gosh – that's terrible," and since *you* are God guess what? Zap... we now have a bad and a terrible, and it is what you created in a blink of an eye just by the judgment you placed on it. There is no bad, there is no terrible and there is no ugly. But, since *you* insist, guess what *you* get? So if you are the type of God who loves to judge and create ugliness and chaos, please do so without involving my Gods who are busy creating love and peace and beauty. Go forth and zap and judge to your hearts content but do not expect to involve others. There is no bad – get this straight. There is however love and through the eyes of love you will see only love.

Let go of fear children. You are wearing fear contacts and you are seeing all through fear. Put in your love eyes and see only love.

Once you began to realize the extent of your nature, you began to look for new ways of seeing reality.

You often took yourselves on long journeys into other realms and even other galaxies. Mostly you wanted to see how you could get unstuck. You became *stuck* by taking on form. Form did not exist until you created it out of vibrational energy. You slowed the vibration of your thoughts until you could "see" your thoughts. Say you wanted a piece of candy. You would "see" how it would look and imagine how it would taste and, voilà! We now have our design. Now we begin to work with design or idea, and slow it down enough to cool it off. You see – to gain temperature, energy must be molded to the proper velocity and then once it is moving at a good speed we stop it dead, and it is now cooling into hardness or firmness. The earth was heated by her spinning and then slowed to almost a stop to harden or firm up.

So, you spun your candy as you would spin a child in the air to play. Only you went such a speed that the "heat" of ignition was set into motion and now we have lift off or igniting of matter. And once you reversed the spin of this matter it began to solidify or take form and shape. This all came about after many experiments and failures on your part. You visualized and your creative ideas took immediate shape and form. You then decided to make an idea into a real perception of what is. You took your real perception of what is and created entire worlds out of it. And to this day you create worlds in other places and *your* perception of what is goes into them and makes them what they are.

If you perceive your world to be dangerous and threatening, your perception is busy at work spinning out other worlds who will see what you see. Please do not create in this fashion any longer. If you see pain and confusion it is simply the pain and confusion that was laid in place by perception and spun to take on life or matter. Life is not real. Matter is not real. What you see is not real. Let go of any polarities. They do not exist. All is put in place by an original perception of what was. What was *thought* is now your reality.

Do not become part of someone's idea. This thought energy is so powerful that you can become what others believe you to be just by consent. Be who *you* are. You are not bad, you are not undeserving and you do not wish to continue this game of creation. Creation is out of control. The biggest problem *in* creation is that she is told to be how she was first perceived. There is a veil of untruth that is put *in* place in each creation and this veil of untruth will surface as truth. Disregard any information that does not "feel" good and right for you. There are many beings on this planet who do not belong here and their truth comes from their own location in space and time. Those who belong on this planet are aware of love and light and they will keep my light shining until you can *all* be recharged and returned.

In other areas of this galaxy and others, there is a plan to re-inhabit earth with those who do not belong on earth. This of course will be accomplished through the procreation process and through alien contact. *This is not to be feared.* This *is* information that will help you know who you are. Do not judge any. Some work with alien beings and still others work with spirits and angels, and some of you even work with God. *I am here to straighten out a few facts in this reality!* I am your father in heaven and I am here to tell you that your warring has gone to far. You are not expected to *claim* this planet or any other. Your place is *in* God, not *in* a cold lump of matter that was formed from someone's idea. Let go of this desire to fight and defend and come out ahead of others, or just on top. You are God. You do not care if you win. It is not good guy/bad guy. That is only illusion.

Stop this nonsense. Love and live as God. Do not judge others as undeserving of God or this Planet. It is all illusion. You are giving power to something that is nothing, or as Liane's mother would say, "You are making a mountain out of a mole hill." Stop giving your power to matter. You are putting your power where it does not belong and this is "sticking" you deeper in matter. Go with the flow. Let everything be. Know that you are God and that *nothing* can really affect God. We must of course remind you that you are so full of darkness and debris at this time that you had best not walk out in front of a train just yet. But your day will come and then you will know the job of being God – a God with no fear. Right now your fears kill you so we'd best keep you away from those you are most magnified or magnetized to.

You will each receive information as you clear that is unbalanced, and this is due to the many areas of work that were done in creation. You may have been a small particle of someone else's past just by association and body connection and therefore you carry this cell memory. You may have been programmed to believe a certain situation occurred complete with dramatics of the situation. This does not mean the actual situation took place. You have been programmed to believe many things and belief is simply thought and thought is creative energy.

If you can hide a "big" truth from yourself such as let's say "I am God," then maybe, just maybe you can change other truths or illusions to suit your own needs. Nothing is ever what it appears to be and often a powerful God will go into denial or even create an old memory that wasn't theirs at all. Some have *no* recall on certain subjects what-so-ever and yet they experienced a situation without recording it. It is all in this game you play. This game is called "Hide God." You are God and you are hiding under many disguises and masks and untruths and this veil of untruth is wearing thin. Those who retain light will be able to see through the veneer of detours that have been set up by *you* to sidetrack *you* in your quest to awaken. Anything to get you riled up so you will attack outside influences and forget about you and what you are really doing.

You are waking and stretching and growing and it is *through* love that you will find God. God does indeed exist and love does indeed exist and soon I will be in a situation that will allow me to show you. You will not wish to create too great a mountain out of what you review as your past. It is not so awesome as it seems. You are playing a very big joke on you by showing you what is; only it really isn't. One thing *is* and that one thing is forever and does not change. It is love. Love sees *all* as equal and treats all as it would be treated.

Go in peace and God bless you "real" good.

*M*ost often it is not necessary to remind you that you are human. You constantly need to be told how human you are so that you begin to *accept* what you have created. If I were to "lord it over you" so to speak, that you are God and look what a mess you have made, you would not wish to hear how this is. So for now, we will say that you are human, creating as God and look what a mess you have made. The only problem with this entire assumption is that it too is incorrect. God did not mess up and you did not mess up. This *is* the plan. Every piece of my big plan is in place and going right on schedule.

So, if *I* created this plan and sent *you* out into *my* creation, how is it that you sit in judgment of me? I do not require your permission to create through you. I require only your permission to enter you. Upon entry I will begin to create in any fashion that I see fit for your particular needs. This is the bottom line.

You do not create out of love at this time as you are full to overflowing with negative thought. This negative thought is creating more negative thought and I do hope you "see" the light soon and "lighten-up" on my creation. Stop judging it to death. Give it a rest! I do not wish you to sit at home in your favorite chair and discuss the rottenness and foulness of this planet.

Liane's mother taught her a very "good" axiom as a child and she tries, unsuccessfully at times, to use it in her adult life. This axiom is to be written down and then pasted on your wall above your sink where you will "see" it and "read" it everyday before you brush your teeth. It goes like this: "If you don't have something good to say then shut up!" Something along those lines is quite good and you get the idea.

I am so tired of not having praise for my work that I could scream. And heaven help those of you who are within hearing range if I do decide to let a roar go! I want credit for creation to go to the light and not to darkness. Stop judging it as black and let it be white. Stop saying "this is bad," and it may just become okay or maybe even good. You do not know why or how or when or what makes it all move, so stop playing God and become God. God does not *judge.* God creates from light and you create from fear. God puts it out there and you color it black and dark and dangerous. Give it a rest! Give danger a rest and give pain a rest.

Judgment is taking over. You see someone kill someone and you scream, "Murder and pain and violence is out there." When you see someone kill someone I wish you to look and say to yourself, "Gee – I wonder how they created that." Not – "Oh boy, another dead cop" or, "Oh boy – another dead gang member," and certainly not "Oh no – this is terrible." No judgments please. Just loving knowledge that these two spirits agreed upon this action and now they are *acting* it out. It isn't even occurring, as everything on this particular level is illusion. *It is not real.* Let it pass. Do not place judgment on situations that you know nothing about. You decide for yourself what is good or bad or right, or wrong, and you pass this information out as if it were law. No more commandments please – I tried that once with you on earth and it did not work. You will use and misuse any information that is set down as a rule or guideline.

It is quite difficult to *give* information through Liane, as it is important to protect her psyche from attack by those who do not agree with whatever I, God, choose to channel through her body. You take my words and you make them fit into *your* creation and so you determine that you have correctly translated God's books, and most of you are so far buried in your debris that you cannot see clearly enough to get the basis of what I am telling you.

You must do enema to clear away your cobwebs and to allow God in. It is simple. Water is inexpensive for most of you, and it takes little time compared to the hours you spend eating garbage and watching debris on television.

How can you "clear" your view when "your" view is distorted by hours of hypnotism provided by a TV screen or by piles of chemical waste obtained from garbage that was never meant as fuel for your consciousness? Your mind needs to unload the garbage it carries. Turn off your TV's. See movies if you must but make certain they are bright and beautiful and loving. *Give peace a chance*, it is not too late. Stop programming yourself to become a destructive machine. You eat and watch what has been proven by many authorities to be harmful... why do *you* think you do not listen?

This is not a good time to bring up the subject of sex, as most often you are frightened by this subject. You are not so much afraid *of* sex. You *are* however, afraid of all that is attached to this simple little game that you play. First of all I wish to inform you that *sex is not bad.* This is of course, contrary to belief and religion and even politics. See, you have begun to fear sex to the extent that you do not allow your political leaders to share sex with anyone but their spouse. "So be it" if this is how *you* wish to live. You make *your rules* and now *you* must live by them.

Stop making commandments and allow every one to be! If one of you wants to have sex ten times a day with ten different people it is okay. None of what you do with sex is of any importance to God. It is no more important than wiping your nose or even picking at it. It is all your personal choice and now you give it so much power that religions form, centered around sex. It's crazy! How did you get so confused about nothing – a bodily function like sneezing or coughing or laughing? All of these function to create and stimulate energy flow within the body. Sexual stimulation will create energy flow within the body. Touch you and you get excited. So what! Touch another and they get excited... so what!

Now, I want you to stop fearing energy. This is the problem here. Energy creates life, and lack or loss of energy creates death. Right now most of you are creating death by shutting down your energy flow. You are taught not to sneeze or cough in public and you are taught not to touch yourself or another in public. Why must *you* have these rules? I want you to think on this while I tell you yet another story.

This story is about a little boy named Tommy. Tommy began to experience pain during sex. He actually loved sex, but the after glow was his problem area. He had lost control. He was man and we all know that man rules planet earth. He began with loving relationships and he gradually grew to conquering in place of loving. So Tommy is now conquering women and feeling quite good about it. Only now he begins to fear his own ability to "make love to" and "please." He begins to believe that in making love he is giving up part of himself and therefore "losing." He is not losing. He just feels as if he is and after sex he is drained and emotionally unwound and relaxed. This is where Tommy created his biggest fear concerning sex.

He got relaxed and was not "on guard" which he believed to be his job. He let himself down by taking part in relaxation and enjoyment and even confused himself by not accepting this as sharing and giving. Tommy began to believe that his partner *took* from him and so he put his guard back up and refused to have sex again. It is not painful to have sex and it does *not* take from you. If you begin to give "fear" so much power and control over you, you *are* going to lose something very good and fun and moving. Do not create pain where there is none. Do not judge sex as anything more powerful than a handshake and we will be back on firm ground where sex is concerned.

You decide what you wish to fear on this planet and you fear out of vision that is distorted. You do not belong in pain and confusion. Imagine my concern as I sit and watch you *destroy* light and turn it to darkness. Stop putting out the light. Give sex its proper and unthreatening place on this planet. You are only touching another body. You came into form to learn to *enjoy* life *in* form. Stop creating blocks and excuses and denial about what you are doing here.

You came here as God to learn to function in matter. You began to experiment with various forms and shapes to the extent that you got trapped in matter out of *your* own fear of not being able to return from matter to God. It is this simple! You went there, I stayed here to give support and share your findings or discoveries. I am watching in horror as you begin to kill off body as you would your worst enemy. Imagine a small child whose parent lovingly creates a party costume. The child puts on the costume to go to his party and all of a sudden this child decides to kill the costume because he is trapped in it. Take off your costume! You are not stuck you are simply *afraid* that you are stuck. It will all be clear to you soon.

It is very important for now that I continue to give information that will calm your fears and get you back on track. Fun and games… that's why we're here. God could not touch or hug without having another. We split and became two so that I might reach around and hug myself.

Woman is not dangerous to Tommy. Tommy is afraid of his own self. When Tommy no longer fears his own physical self he will have accomplished a great deal. It is all up to you how *you* choose to live your life. I will not interfere unless I am requested to do so. My pen requests often and though *she* judges some of my choices for her as painful, she *realizes* that I am setting her *free* of her own fears. Go into *your* fears and watch how they begin to "lighten-up".

Most often you are seen for your mistakes and not for your brilliance, today however we will look at your best side. *You are God.* That is your brilliance. You are God projected to earth and you are life within form. So, how does God project himself to earth? He places thought within each molecule and allows thought or memory to represent him. He is in each and every cell within your body and he is you. You *are* God thought projected to earth.

Now; in the beginning I did not find it necessary to actually "be." It was only necessary to "think" of being. I did not create matter out of thin air. I created from *dense* thought pattern. You are creating at a much denser level than I began at. This of course is due to debris and the result of judgment placed on just about every situation in your lives.

Now; one of the most important parts of this entire process is thought development. Often a thought is born and gradually it develops into a much larger thought or idea and often it is expanded on until it becomes a plan. So, thought is shifted from its original form into what you wish to create according to your own perception of how things s*hould* be. Thought is then dwelt upon and looked at and reviewed and gradually released. This thought now goes out into atmospheric zones and comes back to you in matter.

Things have of course been moving much faster since we began communication, and so we now have creation coming back to you at a much quicker pace. Of course we all know that time does not exist, so what does this "speed up" of time within your dimension mean? It simply means that you are now moving so rapidly in space that you may just catch up with you. This means *all* of you. Alien you, angelic you, monster you and even subconscious you.

Now; we all know that the monsters or dinosaurs are long gone. However, in your mind they are still very real and this of course explains why as a child it was necessary to comfort you in the dark. You believe that something big and bad is out there waiting to get you. This of course is what created Dino's in the beginning. They are not such bad guys, but of course *you* were into creating big and bad.

We all came to earth to create *for* God, so how is it that we now create against God? We are confused! Number one: We do not create for God as we *are* God thought. Number two: We do not really create at all, as we are not *really* here. And number three: You are not human; you are a cell within a cell. You do not exist as a human anymore than a rock does. You exist solely as cell thought. You take on shape and form according to the "thought" that is *in* you. You do not create, you shape and form. Your, or rather "my" thought is what is you and my thought created you and you do not really exist. God is thinking how it will be to be more of himself and "voilà" here you are. I did not wish you to begin to fight me so I created you as equal to me, not lesser than and most certainly not more important than. Just equal… that's all. So what's all the big hoopla about you fearing me? My own thoughts choose to fear their sender? That's pretty drastic or in this case, "imaginative."

You see; God is dreaming and since you are "God in a cell" you receive this image of God's dreams as your own and you create further dreams out of your own Godhood, and now we have the head honcho creating *through* his creation and we have his creation creating through their Godhood. There you have it! God the son is you. God the father is me. Pretty simple stuff really.

So; now we must figure out how God the father puts himself into God the son, then unravel *back* to God the father and become one God again. And how do we figure this out? We look at who we are and retrace the memory cell to see how we were wound or spun into position. In the same way that all life spins and vibrates, you too spin and vibrate. We are now reversing direction, which means that we are backing up by allowing the *flow* to move forward.

We *allow* flow to move by traveling with and not against this flow. And we allow free flow by allowing our stubborn ego to get out of God's way and allow God to take control, and God allows *all* to be without judgments and harsh statements against; and now we have allowed God to take control and we are free flowing and not judging so that we do not stick to any one situation. And this is known to you by now as "let go and let God." You will "stick" only if you judge. Get unstuck or back into life force flow by *allowing* all to be okay. Life is okay.

Do not believe that you die and you will not. It must be programmed into your cell and to program this belief it is necessary to remove old belief on this subject. Old belief says that body must die in order to form new areas or openings for new life to enter. *Not true.* Body is not meant to die ever! So, we begin by cleaning out this old false belief pattern that is buried deep in cells with layers of affirmation on top of it. It has been enforced and re-enforced by death and birth. How often have you heard it said that when Grandpa dies a new child will be born somewhere in the family? So now we must change this to, "When Grandpa travels back to God he will return much better looking!" This is how I wish you to view death. View it through the eyes of love and do not mourn the loss of anyone who dies. They do not die and they do not leave you so please stop this nonsense.

In order to release Liane from her fear of death it was necessary to show her how it felt, and she was astonished at how many waited to greet her as she arrived without body. It's not such a big deal you know. There is no pain in death at all. It is all in your own living mind and it does not exist for those who gave up bodies to float around all day. And as Liane has discovered, they (your dead) are all anxiously awaiting a new body or even just a "hello" from earth. She began to communicate with her brother and others who are there and she soon gave up on that idea. There are so many waiting to be let out, or back into form, that she could not keep up with all the requests to speak with her. You see, not many on earth listen to the dead. Many of you talk to them but you do not listen when they speak to you, and of course why would you? You have enough to deal with right here in this dream.

So, Liane saw and felt death and she no longer fears death and she knows it's not necessary. So now she thinks only of ascension and does not carry "life" insurance, which of course is a *plan* to die and even where you will bury the body in most cases. So you may *plan* to die if you wish but please *know* that it is totally outdated and completely unnecessary.

I will go for now as Liane is tired from writing, but I leave you with this thought. You are but a thought and you think.

You are not to be so surprised that God discusses sex so freely. It is not so important as you make it out to be. Once you learn to treat sex as a handshake, you will no longer "feel" a need for sex. You will wish to see it as no more powerful than touching and rubbing against another. Of course those of you who wish to procreate may wish to continue in this manner of reproduction, until such time as can be elected for us to simply *wish* for a new form in order to *have* a new form. No more having babies after nine months of discomfort and illness and suffering to *bring forth life*. Life is not meant to be suffering, so I wish you to stop judging it so harshly.

Give up your hold on pain. It is not necessary in order to survive. You create more of you, but you do not allow you to enjoy the fruits of your labor. You create pain and guilt surrounding all goodness because you do not believe that you deserve goodness. You are still punishing yourselves for splitting and projecting male and female essence into separate forms. This of course, was discussed at length in my second book titled *No One Will Listen to God*. This is a very good book to reread at this time. That is of course, assuming that you began with Book One, *God Spoke through Me to Tell You to Speak to Him*, and have continued through books two, three, four, five and now of course we are in our sixth grade class with all the intelligence of a twelve year old. Yes, you are "growing" at a good rate of speed. I should have you all back to me in no time.

You will do well to reread all six of God's books as you will learn a great deal *more* in a second, third and even fourth reading. You will only *see* from where you believe. You have *grown* in light and awareness and so you now have the ability to "see" all old information in a new light.

Most of you do not wish to be bored by repetitiveness and I will share some insight into this process with you now. It *is* what makes you "believe." To repeat over and over and over and over is what will teach *all* parts of you who and what you are. If you are too bored to read for this conscious you then I suggest you begin to read for the unconscious you, who is inside of you and *pushing* all your buttons and making you go, or stop. In most cases this subconscious you is very ready to learn and to grow, and with a little push from you he just may get where he's going. He will make a fuss at times and not want to hear what is being read, so I suggest that you allow him to listen while *you* read without placing judgments on what you read.

Of course you will wish to "see" what you have read and at some point it will all become crystal clear. One day you will be sitting with yourself deep "in" thought or creation and you will suddenly *realize* how life really is. It is not so bad as you believe it to be. "Life is a party" and *you* are God's invited guests. You may dance and laugh and sing and love all, or you may stand on the sidelines and judge the players. It is your choice. I didn't make the rules… you did. I simply *threw* the party.

You are not so attracted to being God as you once thought. You are now beginning to "feel" pain at *being* God. This pain comes from confusion that to give up to God is uncomfortable and unnecessary. So, we will begin to show you how you too may become God *without getting in the way of your own Godhood.* You are not the only God here and I do not expect you to "see" others as God until you are ready to accept how *you* are God. You have created enough concern over who is who and what is what, and I will tell you now that *you* are God and *you* are exactly where you are meant to be. You are working at your job and the other Gods are working at their jobs. Each of the cells *within* this body has chosen, out of free will, a job that is their specific area in the healing of God. No man's job is more important than that of his neighbor cell.

You are each asleep at this time and you are walking around doing what you said you would do. Most of you are beginning to wake and stretch and open to light. Most of you are "feeling" change and growing pains. Now; as I have told you prior to this, there are those who chose to slumber up to a specific time and opportunity for their own needs. These sleeping souls do not wish to be upset or pushed at by those of you who believe that your way is best. Mostly these souls wish to be left alone. Their part in this show has not come yet, and for you to push them out onto a stage to do their part now would only create confusion and ruin a very well put together program.

Leave my children alone. I do not need you to push at those who you believe to be asleep or slow witted. They are *not* your responsibility and they do not require your instructions. If a child comes to you and requires care and love, then give care and love not instructions on the "right" or "wrong" of how they live. There simply *is.* I will not allow a wrong way or even an assumption that some will not get back to God. All go. Absolutely every last human, rock, tree, air, mountain and seed will return to God. Nothing *within* God can be left out of God because it is *all* God.

So; if you must create by separating and dividing, then I suggest you do so on your own and *within* your own creation. Do not push your creation on any of my cells. If you do not wish to become a part of this whole, you may go your own way and return in your own fashion. All ways are possible and probable and even real. Do not get so hung up on "one" specific way. There are so many various ways to return to perfection that you would be startled to see all the options.

So; everyone and everything goes. No more changing light into darkness by judging it or coloring it black. This is simply what you choose to paint it and how *you* choose to see it. I do not choose to see my creation as anything less than perfection and I think I may be in a position of higher intelligence than those who scream and complain about how screwed up the world is. I am God and I do not judge you. Stop judging me and my world!

Most often you do not realize how valuable each and every one of you is. You are not to be discouraged by the fact that you are black or yellow or Hispanic or Iranian. All are *God*. No part of God is to be left out of God. There are those who believe that to be white and 'in the know' is what will save you from this planet. It is not what you know. It is not how hard you work at returning to God and it is most assuredly not how *high* you believe yourself to be in the racial department. If you could see you from where I sit, you would give up on the belief that those who are lower class and ignorant are worthless. You do not know how God works, so I suggest you begin to research your own ignorance before you begin to spout off about how certain ethnic races are of no use. All parts of God return to God.

If *you* choose not to see the light or being or God in every person on planet earth, you are choosing ignorance over intelligence. No one is to be put down or criticized or judged as not having beingness. All souls on planet earth are in their correct place and are working on their correct job for God. You do not have my permission to *judge* anyone as not being God. This is final! No one shall tell another who is or is not God. You are *all* God and there are *no* exceptions.

Once you begin to see the error of your own calculations and *how* you created mix-ups in your own universe, you will see how it is *you* that is mistaken on this subject. For now suffice it to say that I, God, am projecting "into" my own creation via this pen in order to straighten out some of the confusion that major teachers are creating. You do good work as a teacher when you teach love and only love. Nothing else exists. No monsters, no computer type controls and no evil. Only love exists and anything else that *you* see is your creation made by you for your own entertainment. Do not teach my children your way if your way is not complete trust and faith based in love – it was never meant to be a test lab and I do wish you would stop turning earth into one by spreading *your truth*. Try to spread God's truth for a change.

You do not wish to be so hard on you. Most often you find yourself wanting to be alone and away from others. This is you wishing to hide from yourself. You do not cope well with who you are and so you escape from you by hiding out. This is how I wish you to learn to cope with your own self, say: "I love you and I will allow you to be whoever and whatever it takes to return to God." This will tell you that you are not judging you.

You will wish to know that to love you is best and to know you may take a great deal of time. My pen often wonders who she is and how she got here and of course I say, "You are God and I sent you out." And this does not help because she cannot "see" how it all works. So she sits in confusion and allows me to move her into strange new areas and strange new beliefs. She is you. The more she moves *for* God, the more God has a foothold in this world or universe.

When you first began to create your world you did not plan ahead and you most certainly did not count on so much fear. Fear is in control whenever you are not working in love. So imagine how often during a single day you are worshiping fear. Most often you see stress and anxiety as a way of life. Stress comes from fear. Anxiety comes from fear. Fear is at the center of all problems. When you let go of fear you will lose your problems. When only love is present you cannot hurt or ache or be confused. It simply is not possible. Love must heal you, simply because you are love and what you are is what you become. You cannot 'not' come home to God. It is not possible to not return. You have no choice. You are a thought; a dream that was sent out and you got stuck but your path is to return full circle.

Liane got to a place in her life where she no longer felt the joy of childhood and the happiness of knowing it's a new day and she could run out and play. She lost her childlike adventurousness and began to look forward to specific events or occasions. If she did not have something to look forward to, she felt lost or bored. So she lost her sense of being in the moment and enjoying the moment.

She began to become unhappy without stimulation of some sort. She needed excitement and adventure. She had to travel and see new places and visit new countries. She no longer saw the dawn of a new day as exciting or the wave of a friendly hand as stimulating. Life began to dull for Liane as she began to fade. Her life light was dimming and she got bored because she was not seeing love. She saw fear and stress and tension and anxiety. She lost her love light and began to turn her body over to fear. Now of course, she "sees" things differently. She wakes and knows how to simply *be* as I have held her "in place" long enough to keep her from losing further love light or life light.

If you too are bored and no longer get a thrill out of a new born day or a setting sun, I suggest you begin to reverse your ways. You are on your way out when you give up your zest for the simplest of pleasures. I just thought you would like to know where you stand. If you stand *in* love, you see joy and exciting life all around you. If you stand *in* fear, you see boredom and stress and tiredness in life.

Let your light shine and your heart sing. Know that you are God and know that you *will* return no matter what. Do not listen to any one who even hints to you that all are not God, because it is not truth – not God's truth. I love you and I wish you sunshine and happiness.

*I*t is not often that an entire group on earth gets to "experience" being gay. This of course, is due to group incarnation and your ability to see ahead to future problems.

So; you got together with your friends and you decided to "come in" as homosexual in order to experience fear of acceptance. So now we have you fearing not only rejection, but also fearing one another. Some of you are so afraid to be gay that you talk as if you are not and you even go so far as to not accept (publicly) those who are gay. I want this to end. No more complaining about what you have chosen as your costume. You are creating "victimization" and it is not a good game. Let go of punishing yourself and let go of punishing others for their choices. This is not a good time to be gay as it is most disturbing for each and every one of you.

So; I suggest you stop being gay! Oh, I see, you have no choice in this "part" you play, so stop complaining and begin to enjoy your role. I do not say flaunt who you are, but please begin to love and "accept" who you are. So what if "they" poke fun – so what if "they" don't understand. Let's let go of all this sniveling and begin to act happy. So what if the big guy's kick sand in your face. You are God and you chose to play this role.

Do you think that you are stupid to select such a painful way to experience? It takes a powerful being to take on powerful lessons. You do not climb the ladder to God slowly when you choose so much at one time. You leap forward in soul "experience" but you must overcome the victimness that you hold on to. Do you not rely on me enough to trust me on this one? If you can learn to enjoy "being" you, you will have won your wings. Do not let outside influences *create* your reality for you. You are God and you may create an entire world of trust and faith just by accepting who you are and knowing that others are only there to show you how you look from the inside.

You are prejudiced against you being gay. If every gay were to see themselves as God and love, we would see an end to gay bashing and "fairy" name calling. No one is responsible for your world and how you see it but you. You are very powerful and loving and kind, so begin to treat yourself with powerful love and kindness.

Now; for those of you who *are* prejudiced against gays or anyone else that you might feel superior to, I wish you to know that you too hate who you are. You do not feel good being you so you mistreat others in an attempt to punish you for being unattractive or stupid or just different. Most often you who bash gays or hate others based on their skin color, are just plain out of body. You have so much self-loathing for your own life that you put down others simply because they live.

Now; I do not tell you this so that you may shout at one another how God said this about gays and God said that about bigots. I tell you this so you might *learn* and *change*. If each of you begins to *see* how you are put together, you will be able to "see" how to unravel this mess and clean yourselves up, or as Liane would say –

"clean up your act." This is just a part that you chose to play and it is not so tough to play it right.

Do not be so certain that *you* are bad. You are not bad, you are not wrong and you do not make big problems by being human. You came to planet earth to be human. Do not judge you for what you are, because you are not even certain of what or who you are. How can you constantly call yourself stupid or unlovable when you don't know how bright and God-like you really are? You are like a bright star that got lost in a cloudy sky. You do not stop being God simply because a cloud comes by and blocks your light. You are most important to God at this very moment.

If you had stayed within God force, I would not have expanded and grown and sought to overcome myself. Yes. God is overcoming his own fear of self. I know this may sound strange and you may misconstrue this to be something other than what it is, but for now I will allow you to see it this way.

So; God began to experiment and wonder and grow and move, and finally part of me got so "moved" by all of this thought pressure; and that part of me began to move and tumble and even "thought" it was falling in space. It did not fall. You believe you were pushed out of God so now you do not like to be pushed around and it is because you remember. You are "pushed out" of the womb at birth and this is simply a reflection of what you *believe* to have occurred. You repeat your beliefs into what you call reality. You begin to believe strongly enough and then your thoughts literally become what you believe. Now; if thought becomes what you believe and has the power to manifest into reality, what happens when you begin to believe strongly in yourself as God? Voilà… God on the rise!

Hence we have God's books telling you over and over again how you are God and how you *are* love, and your subconscious mind after being told something repeatedly begins to believe it, and so what would happen if each person on this planet were to walk around every day saying, "I am God, I am love," until they convinced their subconscious? And how would it be if everyone would just work at love and not at fear? And how would it be if *all* old negative thought programming were flushed down the toilet? And how would it be if an entire planet of beings in bodies began to believe that they are part of a whole God? And since thought creates absolutely everything in existence, how would it be if each being were to return to God with body believing it has risen? Anything and everything is possible if only you believe.

Liane has a hard time understanding how she writes this information, and why her and how did she make this connection, and I will tell her now. You believed you loved God and you believed God loved you and you believed in magic and miracles. Believe and *all* is yours. You may have anything you want if you just begin to change your programming.

See love. See light. Be love and be light. These are my new laws. No other law exists. There is no karma, there is no death; there is no other God. I am here to tell you to believe in love and see the light of God. It is so simple if you could just "see" how simple it is to clear away your pain. You are so *full* of fear that you cannot see the light through the clouds. Remove the clouds and guess what you will see? Do enema and clear this dark cloud, it is simply trapped energy and it must find a way out of you or it will kill another body, and you will float around for awhile and then come into a new body and I must start to teach you all over again. Why not start now? This moment in time could be the first moment ever.

You don't know because you are in a clouded situation, and I see how time does not even exist. You have created many blocks to confuse you. You are so full of debris that it projects out of you in your thoughts and it is creating your life pattern. If you are totally and completely happy with all that you have, with no doubts or concerns, you are living in light. If you have stress or discomfort in any way, shape or form, you are not living in light. I will wish to see everyone in love not in fear. You will know when you are *in* love because you will no longer find others distasteful to you. Not even the drunks who live on your streets. You will have no problem carrying on a friendly conversation or even taking them home for dinner. No fear, no pain, no confusion. To be in love is to "accept and allow to be" without judgment.

Now, don't get confused and think that you must go out and invite a drunken street person into your home. This may not work for you until you have cleared *your* fears. He will reflect your fears back to you, and if you fear being robbed or hurt in any way, guess what *you* may create? Thought has power. Guard your thoughts with your love.

*I*t's not so difficult to begin to see how God does not wish to address big problems. Once I create an opening for discussion, it is most important to forego all desirable results. It is not so important to reach a desired result as it is to clear. Once you have been cleared in a certain area it is most important to fill in that area with new thought or new charge.

You are what you think and you are what you eat. So; if you believe in death and old age and seeing pain and even loneliness, guess what *you are*? How do you know what you believe? Take a good look at who you are. Are you free of problems and do you see your future with enthusiasm and joy? Do you look toward your future and know that only good is waiting for you or do you dread the future and what it may or may not hold? How many of you do not wish to be in the future, and how often have you hated to grow old gracefully or any other way?

Your future is not for you. Your future is meant for God. I will take over from here. You will no longer sit in retirement homes and wait to ascend to heaven or descend to hell. You will be unafraid of all that chains you to life on this planet. In fearing old age, you are fearing your own self. And in fearing yourself you are fearing being you, and to fear you will eventually kill your own self off.

Fear kills and fear destroys and fear causes illness. When you get nervous or angry or stressful, you are in a state of panic. You do not do well with stress and it is becoming your number one killing machine. Stop stress by stopping fear. Fear is easily stopped. Simply give up being afraid. You each have certain situations that are not comfortable for you to be in. These are your fear areas. What you fear is what you will eventually draw. This of course, is based on the laws of gravity and magnetism. If you will let go of these two beliefs, then you will no longer draw what you are. How do you release belief in gravity? Know that there is no gravity and know that you rise, you do not fall. How do you give up belief in magnetism or like attracts like? Let go of this belief and know that you go your way and they go theirs.

Let go of an "eye for an eye" and let go of punishment, because creating revenge will "bind" you to another by magnifying the situation with that individual. *You* have created karma or what you call justice. If you let go of justice and punishment, you free everyone from all situations. You free you and you free them. You no longer *hold* on to another by controlling how or what happens concerning that individual. "Do not get involved" is actually a very smart idea. Whatever you do or say is magnified and becomes part of you to attract more of the same to you. Slug it out or argue it out and you create more of what you have. God does not suggest that you stop defending your right to be, but I do suggest that you allow "all" their right to be. Do not slug it out with them on a verbal level or on a physical level. What you create is something that binds you to that individual. "Let go and let God," unless of course you enjoy being hooked to that particular person for several life times.

So; know you by watching what you fear and know you by watching what you eat. The fear is the magnetic energy and what you digest is the physical energy. Fear is easily stopped by replacing it with love, and food is easily stopped by replacing it with life. It is not necessary to eat and yet you eat to live. You will learn that you do not require food and you will no longer be addicted to certain foods. You require only love. You are love and to ask to be more or less than love is truly ridiculous. So; don't ask for hate and don't ask for vengeance and don't ask for punishment for another. Ask only to be set free of your own fears and you will no longer fall and you will no longer attract what you are, because you will have left what you are and you will be "whole light love."

We have not been good about lack of love on earth. Most often you are so far from love that you feel unloved. We will wish to come full circle and grow in love once again. "In love" is not as you would believe. "In love" is simply allowing all to be who and what they are. It is not so difficult to be "in love" as you believe.

Often you will grow tired of fighting with your loved one to do this or do that, and so you just give up and let them be. Well, give up before you begin. Don't push at and don't convince them to change. Allow them to be and see how you may learn by this situation. Learn to allow everyone to simply be who and what they are and you will see change, big change! You will see a new you and they will see a new you; and they will like this new you so much that they will wish to be like you in every way. Now we have God imitating God or love imitating love. So, how do we get back to God? Live and let live, be and let be, know and let know, or know what you know and let them know what they know.

You will find that it is most difficult to take on responsibility and become responsible for another. When you guide others to the extent that you are telling them how to live, you have taken the role of teacher and student and parent. Don't become attached to others through this process. Each individual is here to learn a specific lesson in a specific area. *You* are here to learn a specific lesson in a specific area. You are not here to teach others how to learn *your way*. You are here to begin to rise up on your own voyage to God and you are here to grow in wisdom. If you continue to teach *your* truth to others, they will begin to learn to be you and not them, or their part. I can't have all my character actors playing the same part. I need all parts to be represented. No changes please.

Inside each of you is the information that will guide you *home*. You do not have to be a quantum scientist to discover who you are or what part you play. You may simply go to your bathroom and put water into your bowels and voilà... a clean machine that spews out clear information! Your body will begin to respond more and more to enema as you release greater amounts of debris. Most of you are so clogged from years of poisons and pesticides and additives and colorings and "stinking thinking," that you no longer function properly.

So, what is proper functioning? Running... in our first three books I asked that you walk. You are in no condition to run at this time. How is it that you have destroyed the body to the extent that you must see a physician before exercising? Exercising is as natural as breathing. You are now told that most of you do not breathe properly and soon you will be told that you must sit and wait to die because your body can no longer induce life from its energy storehouse. And why? Because it's energy storehouse is polluted with drugs and alcohol and preservatives and tobacco and lead and poison and even dirt and grime. Why not put some water *in* you and wash you out. Once you begin to feel clean you will begin to think clean.

Do not be so afraid of water inside the body. It is not natural to be so afraid of something that will clear you and clean you and make you feel good. How can you not want to do this simple, inexpensive technique? Maybe that's your problem. If I don't advertise it as complicated and expensive, I don't get results. Maybe we should keep it a secret, Liane would like that. Then we would have you all writing to say, "How do we get as clear as you" and she could say, "That's my secret" or maybe even, "Well, it's a very special technique and difficult to explain but I'll teach you for a few hundred dollars."

"No price is too steep," you would say. Then you would come to Liane with cash in hand and she would take your money and show you her secret way and you would scream "fraud." You are so afraid, that simplicity throws you off. You are so dirty from the inside that you take millions of dollars in drugs and medication each year. You are so clogged that your heart is stopping and you are having by-pass after by-pass and cutting out parts of you when you could simply clean out your own body. That's all. Take an internal bath. Water is safe. You drink it, you wash with it, you even cook your food in it; so what's the big deal? Maybe fear has taken such a strong hold "in" you that you (the fear you) does not wish to leave. So *you* are now giving your control and your power over to "fear."

Have you read our books and thought, "Yeah, sounds good, but it's not my way." Well, what is your way? Why not convince yourself how you don't need to be cleaned out because your body is perfect and carries no debris and no waste and no chemical preservatives? And while you're at it, convince yourself what a "good" life you're living and how bright and energetic and youthful you are.

You sit there and convince yourself, while Liane and I talk. We'll let you know later what we discuss, because of course you will have convinced yourself that you too can communicate with God so there is no need for us to write these books to you. You go ahead and open to God in your way and we'll see you later….

You are not to be so unaware of who you are. You are God. You are infinite wisdom and joy and love. You are the energy source that is God. You have within you the ability to become whatever you wish. You have simply forgotten your creative power. You once "thought" lake and voilà… we had a lake. You once "thought" human and there stood another human. Just as those who project their beliefs into others, you projected your beliefs into form. You will come to a place in your search for God that is most pleasant. This will be creation… you will remember how you create from thought. Once you are cleaned up and projecting love in place of fear and judgment and guilt, we will *make* a beautiful world together. It is happening now and there is no turning back.

Those who carry great amounts of fear and darkness will not wish to trust the light. This is okay. Do not force *any* to see light until they have been prepared. It is often painful to look at a bright light after being kept in darkness for such a long time. You are not clear at this time and to project your reality on others is just as harmful. You may be projecting what you believe to be reality when in actuality you are projecting old belief patterns. Don't let the old you come out as new information. As Liane once said to a friend, "I don't know who or what I am. I don't know how deep the roots of fear go and I don't know how cleaned out I may or may not be."

Don't be so certain that what you are projecting and teaching is God's truth. There will never be separation of any kind in God's truth. No one gets left out of God as it states in your bible. You do not create so many of yourself and then leave some behind just because you believe them to be unimportant. You are *all* God force energy. How can you not return to God? God is thought; you *are* his thought. Now; when you can understand that one, you will be getting somewhere.

You are creating greater fear on this planet by figuring out how things are and creating explanations for situations that you no longer understand. You once knew how and who you are… but not now. You are asleep. Stop pretending to be aware in this state. Ask questions and learn and *grow* in awareness. Read, learn, listen, feel; take in *all* that is around you. Does it feel good or are you doing what is acceptable? Does your job "feel" good or are you stuck in it. Does your life "feel" good and are you having fun? If you do not create joy in your life, you are not creating from love. You will gradually begin to "see" how you may have joy and not worry. Give yourself time and space to grow into this new you without pain and suffering.

Once upon a time, I did not wish to be seen as villain, and so I began to change. I am God and I do not wish you to believe that I create for you. You have shouted at God with your accusations and pretended that you are not in charge for a very long time. So far the majority of you blame me when you are not happy and ask why I do not help you. I am so tired to being asked to help and being turned away at every opportunity.

I do not force myself on you and I do not judge you for not *accepting* me. You see; to accept me you must *receive* me, and to receive me you must realize that I am you. You must begin to take full responsibility for *your* actions and *your* mistakes and *your* messes. Maybe your mistakes are not really mistakes and you simply do not see the benefit in being in a certain situation. Maybe your messes are not really messes but rather a good measure of where you are and how you have created. Maybe, if you begin to own all that is yours, you will begin to know how to be God.

Maybe you have created great worlds that are often described as God's domain and maybe I do not exist except in your mind and in your heart. Maybe you *are* this entire universe and this would mean that *you* are God. Maybe you are even the only one here and *you* are so big and so vast that you look at other parts of you and what you are seeing is your own body, but you see such a small portion that it looks like a separate cell or human. Maybe you are not separate at all; and if you had a giant telescope you would find that many of you are floating around in this vast body, and you are the one in charge because *you,* a single cell, have the ability and the power to change what *is* in the entire body. So, when you scream at God to fix this or fix that in your life you are telling you to get to work.

You are God and you are this body and you are this force that began it all. Do not be afraid to own Godliness. It *is* who and what you are. You are not here out of chance. You are this giant body that does not wish to be left alone to die. God is alive and well and he exists in every part of you and *you* exist in every part of him. Do not worry that you will not be a good God. You *have* been God since time began and you are just now being told that this is who you are. You are each within God and God *is* within you and you *are* the one in control. Get yourself out of your own mess and begin to control with love. Let go of fear and begin to know how you *are* God.

Watch out for mistakes, correct them and then leave them. Do not hold on to your lessons or you will be holding you back. We are all in this together and we each have our job to do for this Second Coming. You may make mistakes and learn and grow or you may hide in your fear and not take a chance on making messes. I say "go for it." *It* is God and God is you. And the more you learn *who* you are, the more awareness you hold. The more awareness you hold, the more enlightenment you are in.

In enlightenment you will find my pen's favorites; love, peace and happiness. This is freedom. Freedom of choice, freedom of self-desire and freedom *from* self-punishment. When you become "free," you become free from guilt and pain. You may free you from guilt and pain by letting go of judgment. Judgment says right is right and wrong is wrong. Love says, "So what? What is – *is.*" Learn to be free enough to not judge yourself and to give others a second, third, fourth, fifth, sixth and even two hundredth chance. Never quit on you by giving up on them. You may go your own way and stop "pushing" at them to change, but do not go your own way and believe that "they" are a lost cause because "they" are "you" and you are God.

You are so much a *part* of God that you are affecting the entire body of God. You are not so much a part of the vastness as you are an entire organism that is pulsating and vibrating and moving and growing and expanding. You are probably the only whole entity that exists and you are unaware of your own movement and growth and landing and flying and coming and going. You are moving and becoming and shooting off in so many directions that you will one day be unable to see where all parts of you are.

You see; *you* are the God you fear so much. *You* are that giant power that rocks the giant force that got so ahead of itself that the rest of it is still in darkness or sleep state. *You* are the future and the past and the middle. You are now and then and before and after and from now on. There is no end to *you.* You are so big and so extensive and everlastingly beautiful that to see *you* as you truly are would blind you instantly. You must wear blinders as you are waking up to become God. You will be told what you are ready to hear and no more than what you can "see" without hurting your vision.

Your vision is not so much what you see, but *how* you see it. It is you looking at you and seeing you as man or seeing you as God. When you look down at your body, you must see you in order to appreciate who you are. You will not become important by looking down at your own body and seeing nothing but lack of interest or distaste. You must become important to you in order to save you. You are not willing to save someone who is of no value, so we must get you to see the value in you. *You* are everything because you are all that exists.

Now; when you begin to know you a little better, you may even begin to know how you fit in and believe yourself to be valuable. Once you are convinced of your own value, you will see how others are also *part* of this whole and once you see others as part of you, you will be seeing how God is simply one body with several minds and arms and legs and eyes. God contains so many cells and atoms and molecules and original parts and old parts that you are confused as to who and what you are. So now we are putting *you* in your right place, and once *you* learn how you fit in, others will follow automatically.

It is law that like must attract like and until this law is broken, you will draw the *rest of you* to the light just by *being* in light yourself. Your tail or head (if you are the tail) will follow wherever you go because it is all you following you. You are this giant centipede that is all connected and you are beginning to wake up and go home. You do not have to wake the rest of you and you do not have to retrace your steps. You may simply come home and surrender to God what is God's.

When you ask to become "light" and "wake up!" you will see a whole new world. You will turn-on your love channel and no longer "view" darkness and fear. Fear rides constantly with you but you are learning to *dissolve* fear by turning "on" your love light. Light will always cast a new perspective on a dark room and it will cast a whole new light or view of this planet. Light goes on… dark disappears. It's just that simple! Let go of your fear – do not hold on to a position you do not care to be in because your fear is stopping you from moving. Movement is very necessary at this time.

As you begin to move to the light you may be afraid. You may lose a few well meaning friends. You may also lose you… the old you. And this can be most saddening and the loneliest of all. To be alone and missing you, because you do not exist any longer. The old you is gone and a whole new you is sitting here and you don't know how to handle this "new you" or even how you lost the "old you." You will however continue, and wonder why. It is because you must go to the light. You are being drawn and the choice is already in the works. Light will live. Darkness will die. You will live as God and you will die as evil. No evil exists. It is not possible. It is all in the blink of an eye or the "view" of a moment.

You will change as if turning to a new channel on your T.V. Out goes the bad stuff, on comes the good stuff. Out goes death and destroying and on comes health and loving. You will each be drawn because you are each part of this giant centipede that is stretched around this planet. I suggest you re-read Book Two, *No One Will Listen to God* if you do not remember how the centipede works.

So, know the value of you and you will begin to accept and admire your own position in God's body, in accepting and admiring you, you will be accepting and admiring God. God will then be acceptable to you. You do not return to God at this time because *you* refuse to accept that *you* are indeed God. This is good for now.

So now you are finding it difficult to find "you." You are trying to identify yourself and be who you believe you should be, when in actuality you *are* who you are regardless what you believe yourself to be. So; if you are God and you have a tough time accepting this fact, it does not change or alter the fact that you are. You will believe yourself to be whatever it is that convinces yourself that you are this particular identity, but in reality you are God; and the idea of being God is so threatening to you that you begin to squeal and squirm and carry on like you do not know who you are or how you fit in. You are not meant to be so important that it frightens you to be who you are. You have placed so much emphasis on God that no one wants to be God. You are meant to be royalty, but what you have done is to convince yourself that God is untouchable, unreadable and unlovable.

You are being taught to *fear* God! No one believes God would communicate and no one believes God is good and loves you. Oh, you are told how "God loves his children but only if they are good." No one is told that "God is happy when you are bad," so now you believe yourself to be undeserving of God's love because you know how you do not handle being good very well. You spend the majority of your time being bad (in your view), but we all know by now that no bad exists. We are each God and we each do no wrong. We are on our way to Godliness and "accepting" our Godliness. So now you must begin to show how you *are* God even though you do not "feel" like God.

We will get you to a point that is most advantageous for you to begin to accept who you are. You are not to be so concerned at this time with who *you* believe you are or how you believe you fit in. All will fall into place for you to take on your role as God. No fear is required and I do suggest that you take this role of God in stride. It is not so important to be God as it is to allow God to be you.

I have taught Liane to ask me to be her, and this helps her integrate the God-self with the human-self. She has asked repeatedly for God to be her and this is like an open invitation for me to enter her. She is constantly working at being God and I am doing my best to convince her that she need not work at being what she already is. She is now in a position that is very good for her and she will be very good with "accepting" God and "becoming" God. You too will become God and you too will learn to simply let *you* be God.

It's not so difficult as you believe. Just get out of my way, and of course, to get you out of my way it is important to move you to the light. To move you to the light, it is important to "be" who you are long enough to show you the way to the light. To be who you are, you must allow you to "be" and stop judging yourself as "not good enough," or "too bad" to be God. You will learn some day that you do not have a chance when you fight being God. God will get you, because you *are* God and it is only your belief that you are not that keeps you from opening up to who you really are.

So far we are doing very well with our lessons. Change is becoming more and more acceptable and love is spreading out of control. Most of you are finding it very difficult to stay angry for long, and forgiveness is on the rise. God is sneaking *in* to this dimension and darkness is becoming weak. All is well and all is right. I will wish to see you all accepting and receiving God soon.

No one is allowed to stay outside the God force for long. This dimension is moving and responding well. Most of you have been stuck in matter for such a long time that you are no longer *aware* of your connection to God. Once you begin to *see* how you are God, you will be "free" to become God once again.

So far you do not believe that you are God, so we must now convince you. This of course, is not going to be easy. Both Liane and I get tired of pushing information *through* her body. She has been an overly eager pen at times and her body has given out and even collapsed into exhaustion at times. She just does not want to quit and she does not want to let you down. See; she believes that her soul's purpose on this plane is to communicate for all who wish to open to this information. So she communicates and she loves this work for God, even when it knocks her off her feet for short periods. She is not accustomed to being a channel, as she has not studied this technique nor has she studied metaphysics or psychic training. She just asked and I just answered.

She still asks, "Why me?" and I still say, "Because you asked." And of course, she is not too satisfied with such a plain honest answer. After all, she is surrounded by those who have studied such phenomena for years, and they have asked, so "why not them?" I will let you in on a little secret... *believe* you can and guess what? You really can. She believes what I tell her and her simple, uncomplicated trust allows her to create miracles.

Let go of being better than, or on top of, or one in the know, be simple, be open, be love, and be you. Don't worry how you look to others and don't worry how others *view* you. You are God and you are creating for your own God-self. You are not creating for them and you are not responsible to them and you are not to answer for them. Answer for you, know you and be simple. Let go of being right and confess how you know only from your own position and you do not know how long you will hold your current position. You can *view* reality only from where you stand.

If *you* have created a world of mistrust and hate, *you* will see pain. If... *you* have created a world of love and faith you will see beauty, and if *you* have created a world of peace and harmony *you* will see "peace." Know who you are and "look" at *your* world and accept responsibility for it. For in accepting responsibility for *all* that you have created, you will allow *you* to change the world you now perceive. You will most easily change a world picture by owning your own creation and allowing it to "be" without judging it to death.

Do not kill off old belief systems or views. Allow them to be – without pointing and saying "this is wrong" – and you will have a much easier time "changing" what you are viewing. A view is simply a position that you have taken or your stand on any particular subject. Do not place your point of view in a position of judgment. Allow your "view" to change and soon you too will be creating miracles and communicating with me. It's no big deal you know? I am you, so it's a good idea to get to know me, and I'll tell you all about you just as I have with Liane. She asked and I said "Yes, it's time I intervened and show my children how to be God again." I am God and I wish to communicate with *all* parts of myself. Liane is a good place to begin, but I wish to communicate with *all* parts of God not just a few.

I will communicate with those of you who ask, and you may believe your answers to be given to yourself by yourself, but I assure you that you are God and when God speaks to you it "feels" like part of you speaking or writing to you. I will work with you through your fears and I will show you your path as I have with Liane. It all gets easier as we go.

I have opened a great hole in this dimension, and with the consent of my pen I entered and I began to *clear* a larger space for myself by way of her form. She is not the first to give herself over to God. She is however, one of the few to go public, and "open" to larger numbers the information that is necessary to open huge outlets, or rather inlets, for God to access himself in matter.

God had to sneak in and communicate with himself *in* matter, because the portion of God who is in matter is so afraid of God and who or what God is, that he cannot freely communicate with his own self. So; God answered Liane because she was unafraid in certain areas and because she was gullible! Yes, you who are afraid to be gullible will have a hard time swallowing information given to you by you (God). You are too clever and on guard, so no one has a chance of tricking you.

Liane is easily told to do what "feels" good and right *for her.* And because it "feels" okay, she goes easily into new areas, and of course she has been prepared to play this role for you. She is just one of a few who are courageous enough to go blindly where no human has before walked. She doesn't "feel" courageous but she is none the less. So, now you know… simple minded is not such a bad way to be. Sorry Liane… no pun intended!

You are so afraid to be alone that you reach out and "grab" on to anyone or anything for support. This is how some of you become followers. You do not wish to be you so you give your power over to another and you allow them to tell you how to live and how to think. So far you have been balancing to the extent that you will not wish to be alone. You are learning to depend on you and to not "lead" others into your belief or your world.

Let my children believe whatever they wish. You are to be concerned only with your own self. Do not begin to push this information as others have done with your bible. These books are being written to teach those who are open to this line of thinking and it is not necessary to push them at folks who do not wish to hear. We have a great deal of work to do and most of this work is for *you*, not them. Concentrate on you and not on them. Don't push, don't follow, just be. Be you – the best you that you know how to be. And when you slip or fall, do not curse you or judge you. *You* are God, so no swearing at God please.

Now I wish to discuss creation. Once upon a time I began to separate myself in order to "feel" who or what I was and am. I did not investigate out of "judgment" that I must be more, but simply out of "curiosity" of my own vastness. I began to contain any curiosity that went into my own self-awareness or self-discovery, and now of course I contain huge amounts of curiosity, since you are all me and we are all very curious as to who and what we are. Most often I began to grow the instant I had thought. I had thought the instant I had an awareness of being, and I had awareness of being the instant I woke up to be. So; when did I wake up, and does being asleep mean that I did not exist in thought form? What is thought form and how did it start and where did it come from? Most often thought *is*. It is an idea when you believe or use it, but where did it originate? I believe that thought is plasma; that thought is what we breathe and what we eat and what we are.

I believe that to think is to live and when you give up thinking you die. The energy that creates is thought. The energy that is love is God and God is thought. You may change you back to God by simply thinking and believing strongly that you *are* God. It is all illusion and yet it is what *you* make it. God is real, but what *is* reality and who decides? We have much to learn and much to discuss and we are all curious about how we got here. So; be patient and we will learn and grow as we go.

This is especially meant for Liane, since she is "pushing" herself to do more and channel faster. She has slowed down her rate of writing these past two years and it is due to the pain involved in channeling this bigger or faster vibration. She thinks maybe she's not as good at this as she once was, but she is simply working at a much faster pace on another level. The body can only take so much God force at once, because the body is energy in matter and matter does not really exist. So when I push through Liane's body, her body sends out warning signals that she is destroying it. She is! She is destroying the illusion of matter and so her body fights me and I always win and she receives big signals from body saying how beat up and exhausted she is. This is due to the level she now works at.

In the beginning, she actually felt energized after she channeled. This was due to the low frequency vibration that stimulated "life" in her. Now we have reached a level that is beyond gentle stimulation and she is concerned because it no longer "feels" good to channel. It stirs up debris and emotions and her body is easily fatigued by all this fuss over God shaking and moving.

You too may reach this level where you no longer feel you have the strength to continue. Don't worry. God will not let you fall. You must rest when you must and this too is good.

Originally there was no light. Not that light had extinguished, however light *had* evaporated to the extent that you did not believe in a God of any good. You were raised to believe in a God who killed and maimed and was offered sacrifices. Now you believe in a God who is unjust and punishes you for being bad. So far we have restored very little faith and trust in a loving, kind, faithful God. Yes; faithful is not how you see me. You believe that I will leave you the moment you are what *you* call bad. *I do not leave you ever.* I cannot leave my own body and go out into never-never land when *I* exist as everything.

I am not so much you as you are me. You are the part of God who sits in judgment of your own self. You will begin to see how you are controlling you through guilt and judgment. Once you begin to wake up to the fact that wrong does not exist, you will give yourself a much needed break. Most often you are in a position to see all as not good, when in actuality, all is good and well. You judge because you are being pushed or moved to change, and to change is most difficult for you. You do not trust movement without prior knowledge of the hows and whys and wherefores. So now you sit and say, "Oh, I must be a bad person because this or that has not gone well for me." And in actuality, this or that has gone *extremely* well, because you were *moved* into a new area or *fear.*

Fear, all fear, must dissipate in order for God to wake up on planet earth. You do not know who you are so stop judging your life as undesirable. Live only in the moment and let go of any preconceived ideas of what may or may not be good for you. If it is occurring to you or for you now, it is best. It will move you and shake you up enough to set you in a direction that will guide you into a new way of seeing. When you begin to see "all" through eyes of love, you will be seeing all clearly. Love does not judge. Love does not protect nor defend. *Love is.*

Love simply allows all to be whatever form is necessary. Love does not jump up and scream at you to stop being stupid. You make the rules as to what is stupid and what is smart. You change fashion to "dress smart" and when everyone begins to dress smart you decide to change fashion and call them outdated and old fashion. You will not create in this manner forever, so don't get too attached to it. You have had many outdated ideas and books and thoughts that you now look back on and laugh.

Begin to laugh now! Stop being so serious about an existence that is only a dream. Lighten up!! Lighten and brighten and spread joy. This game of ignorance and deception is just that; a game, nothing more, nothing less. Stop hurting yourself over a silly game. It's not important. Life as you know it does not exist and you are here to become what you are hiding from. You are stuck so far down in your own "belief" of guilt and judgment that I can't get you to stop beating your own self up. Once you begin to release judgment you will allow you to be. Once you allow you to be, you will be free of tyranny and vengeance.

I am not a vengeful God and I do not wish you to reap vengeance on yourselves. Knock it off! Get down off your cross and give up punishment. You are God and your own *power* of judgment has created this belief *in* you. Give an idea power and it will become so. No one is created from light or you would all have risen off this planet by now. Give your power to a word or an idea and since you are God... *it will be!*

Stop creating pain and judgment and a belief in wrong and right. Be God. Do not be wrong and do not be right. Do not be good and do not be bad. Just be who and what you are and *move* when I move you. It may *feel* painful but it is really the end of pain or the beginning of the end of pain. You will not wish to feel pain in your future, as pain is caused by punishment and punishment is dealt by you, to you. Stop punishing you by putting you in stressful situations. A situation is *never* stressful without your consent. If you see it as fun and games it becomes fun and games. Some people love crowds, others believe crowds to be noisy and pushy and outrageous, and they freak out and have stress. So; is the crowd bad or is the individual creating unnecessary stress for himself.

Your entire life is based on this system. See all as good and you begin to live in "Good." You are creating your own stress by your own *view* of your world. Change *your* perspective and change your world view. You control your entire view of how you see all. No judgment. No death. No pain. Know it. Believe in it and let go of all else.

You are carrying excess baggage and it is too heavy and creating more pain and discomfort. Put down your load and feel free to fly. I will want you each to unburden yourselves for our rise off this planet. It is going to *be*, as I am the one being born and I will not be denied. God is coming to earth on a wing of flight and a prayer of hope.

One little girl has gone deep enough into her fear to "lighten the load" for many. She is afraid and alone but she does not quit. She is you and you *are* ready. Now is the time to rise up and begin to float free of the weight that holds you in place on this plane. You will walk tall with hope in your heart and know that God does indeed communicate with his children.

You are lost and confused and I am gathering you up to send you home. Home is light and home is God and God is all that exists. No evil. No devil. No Satan. No computer type controls over you. Only your belief in such enemies creates blocks for you. You will rise and you will dissolve the other thoughts that have created walls of fear. Others will follow and each part of God will be "sucked" back into God – one at a time, then two, then three, then more. And very soon I will have each and every part of myself back where we began. Not back in place, because you never left. You blasted off into space only you are space. So; part of you is zinging around believing it is lost but it is just out of touch with reality. This is God's reality and it is best to know God's reality.

Wake up and see a bright new tomorrow. You are on top and going higher. You are the one who wrote this to you. You are tricking you into submission and fear and darkness. Don't give up. Part of you is awake and writing back to you through this girl to shake you out of your sleep. Wake up now… come on… get up… look around… it's not how you thought it was… it's much, much better!

Now I wish to discuss rape. So far you are unaware of the power you have divined toward the act of sexual intercourse. Most often you are totally unaware of your own body and how it functions. Rape is a response to neglect in the body. One's body forces build to such a screaming point that release is inevitable. The person who rapes is driven by his or her own body need. He may feel euphoric or simply let down after such a violent release. So; why should someone who does not receive great thrill out of molesting or raping continue to act so selfishly? I will answer these questions and more in our future books.

So far no one is in tune with their own body needs and this is very important once we begin to adjust to the idea of ascension. Most often the body is left completely in the dark as to what is next for it. It sees through eyes that reverse the image and even turn it upside down. All is done to confuse the body. The body is not trusted by the "being" or "soul," so the communication is under developed to say the least. No one tells 'body' how to ascend when your "being" goes home at death. No one communicates to God *directly* through body. God works through spirit and spirit controls body and suggests that body is not so good looking and not so smart and not so lovable.

So; body breaks down and begins to lose interest in living and now we know how we kill ourselves. We judge ourselves to death with words and important rules to keep us under control – "no one is looking out for you but you." – "no one loves you but you." You say this to yourself until you begin to know it as a truth and then you tell body how ugly it is or how fat or how stupid; and because *you* have already convinced your body that you are the only one who will take care of it, it begins to see how that's too bad – since *you* don't like you very well.

So; we have a great deal to learn and a great deal to share and even more to express to our "real" selves. So far we have just begun… I am leaving now for a much needed rest. Liane has done far too much and I wish her to let her body come back into balance. She has seen a great deal and experienced on many levels, and now I am asking her to take a long rest in order to allow her body the time it requires to adjust to the new light it *receives*. She has taken on great amounts of light in a short period of time and she has not the sense to stop this work on her own so I am stopping it for her.

You are now at the end of book six. "The Survival of Love" is just exactly that. Love must survive in order for light to be present. Once light is present, the darkness disappears. And once the darkness is all gone we will love as love is meant to be. So far you are far too attached to belief systems and ideas to know anything about true love. True love does not judge nor does it paint a sad love story. True love is acceptance of one's own self and denial of anything that even suggests that the self is not a perfect human being.

You are each God coming home to God. My prayers are with you as *you are* me in action. God's thought is being rolled back into itself in order to return God to God…

The end for today!

God's Pen

I first heard the voice of God in 1988. I was sitting in my back yard reading a book when this big booming voice interrupted with, "I am God and I will not come to you by any other name." I felt like the voice was everywhere – inside of me as well as in the sky around me. I was so frightened that I ran in my bedroom to hide.

This was not the first time that I heard voices. I had been communicating with my own spirit guide or soul for about a year. I guess my depth of fear regarding God, and all that he represented to me at the time, was just too much.

I spent two days trying to avoid the voice of God, which was patiently waiting for me to respond. By the second day I was exhausted from lack of sleep and decided to give in and talk with him. This turned out to be the greatest gift and best decision of my life.

The first book, *God Spoke through Me to Tell You to Speak to Him*, shows my evolution from communicating with my soul to communicating with the Big Guy. It took a couple years for me to be comfortable communicating with God. My fear of a punishing God was big! That has most definitely changed and I now think of God as my partner and best friend.

In the beginning the voice of God would wake me in the middle of the night and tell me it was time to write. He said I had promised to do this work (I assumed he was talking about the soul/spirit me). I would drag myself up to a sitting position and watch in amazement as my hand flew across the page, while I tried to keep up by reading what was being written.

It was always so much fun to wake up the next morning and grab my notebook to see what God had written during the night. After some time the voice stopped waking me and I became comfortable picking up my pen and writing for God first thing in the morning. I think in the beginning I had to be awakened while still semi-conscious from sleep so I wouldn't object too much to the information that was being channeled through me.

As I grew less and less afraid (and more trusting) of God, he was able to communicate greater information. Some of the information is quit controversial, but I felt it important to just let it be and not censor it. I present the writings here to you as they were given to me. I have edited a little (mostly the more personal information regarding myself) and I have used a pen name for privacy reasons. I asked God for a good pen name and he guided me to Liane which (I was told) in Hebrew means "God has answered."

At one point I became a little concerned about my sanity in all this, so I went to a hypnotherapist to find out what I was doing. Under hypnosis I saw this incredibly huge beam of light with a voice coming from within it. It was a giant "loving light" and felt so comforting and kind. It felt like that's where I came from. After that I stopped worrying about my sanity. If this is crazy, I think it's a very good kind of crazy to be....

In loving light, Liane

Loving Light Books

Available at:
Loving Light Books: www.lovinglightbooks.com
Amazon: www.amazon.com
Barnes & Noble: www.barnesandnoble.com

Also Available on Request at Local Bookstores

www.ingramcontent.com/pod-product-compliance
Lightning Source LLC
LaVergne TN
LVHW011356080426
835511LV00005B/319

* 9 7 8 1 8 7 8 4 8 0 0 6 4 *